You Thought You Knew

You Thought You Knew

By Kevin Federline

Published by Listenin™ Inc.,
in association with Barracuda Baby Productions Inc.

Listenin

This work is published under exclusive license to Listenin Inc.

Published by Listenin™ Inc., in association with Barracuda Baby Productions Inc.
Delaware, USA

First edition, 2025

ISBNs:
Hardcover: 979-8-9996125-0-2
eBook: 979-8-9996125-2-6
Audiobook: 979-8-9996125-1-9

For rights and licensing inquiries: info@listeninbooks.com

www.listeninbooks.com

@listeninbooks

Listenin™ is a trademark of Listenin Inc. Trademark registration pending.

INTRODUCTION

I've been back and forth on doing this book for years. Thought about it. Let it go. Picked it back up. Jotted down thoughts in my phone more times than I can count. Memories, fragments of what I'd say if I ever really sat down to do it. But I always stopped short. The timing never felt right. My kids were still young, still finding their way through a world that was already heavy on their shoulders. I didn't want to make it heavier. I didn't want to stir shit up when they were the ones who'd feel it most. So I waited.

Now they're older. And I'm ready.

This is about finally telling my story. My version. In my words. Because everybody else has done it for me. The media. The blogs. The exes. The strangers. The jokes. The headlines. They all had something to say about me. And I stayed quiet. I took it. I didn't correct the record. I didn't fight back. Not because I agreed, but because I was trying to protect the people I love. Trying to give my kids some kind of normal life. Trying to avoid adding fuel to the fire.

But silence didn't bring peace. It left me choking on the words I never said.

I've carried this for a long time. And if I'm being real, part of me thought maybe I'd never say anything. Maybe I'd just ride it out and let the story be what it was. But as my kids get older, I see it differently. I don't want them growing up feeling like they have to explain who their father is. I don't want them defending shit they never lived. They didn't ask for any of this. If people want answers, let this book carry them.

Because I want my kids to know: their dad told his story. And he told it with truth.

And yeah, this is for me too. I've carried a lot. Stuff I never processed. Moments I never made peace with. This book has cracked all that open. It's made me look back and see things differently. Some of it hurts. Some of it heals. But every word of it is honest. And at this point in my life, that's what matters most. After two decades of everyone else telling the world who I am, who wouldn't want to finally tell their own story?

CHAPTER ONE

Becoming a dancer wasn't something I planned. It was something that found me. As a kid, I loved to move. No formal training, no structured lessons, just me and the music. Back in the '80s and '90s, hip-hop was taking over, and I fell right into that wave. It was more than just a genre of music; it was a culture that consumed me.

When I was thirteen, I had a girlfriend who danced at a local studio near my house in Fresno. I'd walk over to see her during breaks or chill with friends working at the Subway next door. That's when I first noticed this group of guys at the dance studio. They weren't your typical dancers doing jazz or ballet. This was something different. It was a crew, six or seven guys, all older than me, maybe fifteen to twenty years old. They were doing routines similar to what I'd seen on TV, and I couldn't stop watching. It was so dope, and I wanted in.

Eventually, I joined them, and the dance studio became my second home. At the time, it was rare to see an all-male dance group in a studio setting, especially in Fresno. It was groundbreaking. We entered big competitions in L.A.—and won. Every. Single. Time. We were something new, something not many people had seen before. I stuck with that crew for a couple of years, but by fifteen, I got sidetracked—teenage distractions, street shit… more on that later.

By nineteen, I'd been through a lot, but dance never left me. I heard that Dwayne, the guy who led our crew at the dance studio, had started a nonprofit called Dance Empowerment. It was all about bringing kids off the streets and giving them a chance to learn dance through grants and funding. His dance studio was right down the street from my apartment. One day, I walked in, and that's when I saw Jimmy Federico again.

Jimmy had been dancing at the studio since before I left four years earlier. Now, he was a beast. I was blown away by how good he was. Seeing the progress instantly reignited something in me.

I thought: *I've wasted time, but I can still get better. I can still be great.*

Jimmy became my motivator, my competition, and quickly my best friend. I joined Dance Empowerment and trained like my life depended on it. For two years, it was all about learning, growing, and perfecting my craft. Jimmy and I became inseparable, pushing each other every day. He was already making moves, signing with an agent after being spotted at a competition in L.A. He even landed a spot in Christina Aguilera's first music video, *Genie in a Bottle*. When he came back from that shoot, he couldn't stop talking about it. The excitement in his voice, the stories he told about the experience—it was infectious. That's when I realized I had to get to Los Angeles. Soon after, Jimmy and I made a few trips to L.A. to take classes from top choreographers. The first time we went, driving over the Grapevine and descending into the city, I had this overwhelming feeling like: *This is where I'm meant to be.*

Someone had suggested we take a class with Wade Robson. I heard Michael Jackson had discovered him, so we checked out his class. It was the hardest class I'd ever taken, but at the same time it wasn't really my style. Back in Fresno, Jimmy and I were some of the best. In L.A., we were small fish in a massive pond. It was humbling, but it made me hungry. Jimmy had met a dancer named Andre Fuentes on one of his trips to Los Angeles. Andre was already dancing for major artists at the time, and he offered us a place to crash. He only had a one-bedroom apartment, but he was always about helping other dancers. His place was a revolving door of aspiring talent. People were crammed into every corner, but we didn't care. We were young, broke, and chasing a dream.

When we were finally settled, we hit the ground running. I auditioned for every dance agency in town. It was brutal, open calls with hundreds of dancers from around the world, all fighting for the same spot. Rejection became my daily routine. I'd go back to Andre's apartment, questioning if I had what it took.

Then, one night, everything changed. I was out at a club, blowing off steam, just dancing like I always did. You see, the difference with the club scene back then—it was a vibe for dancers. There wasn't any bottle service or VIP sections. Everyone came together, no matter your status. You fed off the energy from the people around you. At times, it almost felt tribal. I thrived on it. A man approached me on the dance floor. His name was Brendan Filuk, and he was an agent at DDO, one of the agencies that had rejected me. He told me, "I want to represent you. Come to my office tomorrow."

I was like, "You guys just told me to fuck off the other day."

He said he wasn't there and didn't care.

The next day I walked into his office, and he offered me a contract. He told me he was leaving DDO to set up his own shop, Bloc Agency. At the time, I had no idea that it would go on to become *the* dance agency representing the biggest names in the industry. All I knew was that someone finally saw something in me. From that point on, everything fell into place: auditions, bookings, gigs. I was finally doing what I loved, what I was born to do. Dance wasn't just a passion. It was my way out. It was my therapy and my purpose. It saved me from a path that could have led to a much different destination.

Dance taught me resilience and how to grow in the face of rejection. It gave me a life I never could've imagined back when I was just a kid watching dancers in a studio. For me, it all began with a little hip-hop crew in Fresno and a desire that refused to die. Becoming a professional dancer wasn't something I fully understood when I arrived in L.A. It was a whole different world. Auditions were intense: you'd walk in, learn choreography on the spot, then perform, sometimes against hundreds of other dancers. They weren't looking for someone who'd eventually figure it out; they wanted a machine, someone who could absorb choreography instantly and execute it to perfection. I wasn't quite there yet, so I had to adapt quickly.

Within two weeks of moving to L.A., I had an agent. Two days after signing, Brenden got me into a small, closed audition with about twenty or thirty guys. They were looking for four dancers to join a tour for LFO, a boy band opening for Britney Spears. I wasn't polished enough to stand out in the choreography portion, but auditions often included a freestyle section, and that's where I shined. Freestyling let me connect with the music on a different level, and it showed. Somehow, with a little help from my agent, I booked the job. The choreographer was Ed Moore, someone I'll never forget. He gave me a ton of guidance in a brief span of time and was incredibly patient while I found my footing. I remember during rehearsals, Ed lined up pennies on the floor that I had to scoot with my feet to help me nail a step I was struggling with. I had a few moments like that, rough but expected. Still, the feeling was indescribable: years of hard work and passion finally paying off.

Calling my parents to tell them I was going on the road was a surreal moment. They knew I'd moved to L.A. chasing a dream, but hearing that I'd booked my first gig made it real for them. For me, it was validation. After two weeks of rehearsals in L.A., I was on a plane to Florida to start rehearsing with the band.

The tour kicked off in Pensacola. We had about a week to prepare. Walking into that arena for the first time, seeing the massive stage, and knowing I'd be performing in front of tens of thousands of people was a rush. The adrenaline, anxiety, and excitement hit me all at once.

All I could think was: *Don't screw this up. Don't be the one to mess up on stage.*

The four dancers—Brian Friedman, Make B, Sherman and I—quickly became a squad. Brian and Make B really showed me the ropes since I was the rookie. They let me know I'd be getting the most shit. Tour life was brutal but exciting. You lived out of a suitcase, constantly moving. Planes, buses, arenas. Everything moved fast, there was no room for error.

That first performance was unforgettable. The lights, the crowd, the *energy*—it was everything I'd imagined. But the late nights, the early mornings, and the pressure to deliver every time hit hard. And then there were the off-stage moments, like the time I stayed out all night with a girl in Pensacola, watching plankton glowing in the surf, only to show up late for the bus the next morning. The tour manager ripped into me, making it clear that being late wasn't an option. Lesson learned.

Life on the road with LFO was an experience on and off the stage. They were wild, pulling stunts that were *Jackass*-level.

It was bizarre, but they were good guys at heart. They had their moments of craziness, but they also lived to perform, and I could relate to that.

The bus rides were where the real memories were made. Nine of us—dancers, LFO, and crew—crammed into one bus. Late-night video games, endless conversation, and lots of laughter made the long drives bearable. Tour buses became a second home.

As for Britney, we didn't cross paths very much. She was sixteen, and I was twenty-one. That's a much bigger gap at those ages. We were worlds apart. She didn't even remember me when we connected years later. Most nights, after our set, we'd watch some of Britney's performance to show some love to the other dancers, but we rarely stayed for the whole show. If we had to head to the next city, we'd leave early. Otherwise, we'd hit the town, always looking for the next party.

The first leg lasted three months, mostly along the East Coast. From Florida, we worked our way up, and eventually made our way back to L.A. By the time it ended, I was exhausted but fulfilled. I'd saved almost every penny I earned. Between per diem and paychecks, I didn't have to spend a dime on the road. Per diem back then was $350 a week, which covered more than enough. On top of that, we were earning $1,500 to $2,000 a week. By the end of the run, I realized I was making more money than I ever had in Fresno.

But that first tour was more than just a job. It was an education, an adventure, and the start of a journey I'd never trade for anything. I learned how to perform, but more so how to survive in a world that demanded resilience and adaptability. From packed arenas to rookie mistakes, every moment proved dreams come true—if you're willing to work.

Returning to L.A. felt like a reset.

I was ready for the next challenge, but there was uncertainty. LFO's management had planned another leg of the tour, but they were only bringing back two dancers. The rest of us didn't know if we'd make the cut. It was nerve-wracking. This was the reality of the industry: you could be on top one day and back to hustling for gigs the next.

CHAPTER TWO

After returning from the LFO tour, I was coming into my own. The grind, the constant auditions, and the whirlwind of experiences had started to shape me. My confidence was building, but there was still the looming question: *What's next?*

Back in L.A., my buddy Jimmy, who I'd moved with, had started booking some solid gigs, including getting ready to go on Mandy Moore's tour. We didn't see each other as much since we were both grinding, but we had the same goal: save enough money to finally get our own place. The one-bedroom apartment we'd been crashing in, with five people rotating in and out, was getting old. Luckily, Brian Friedman let me use his place for a while. He and Andre were going out for the final leg of Britney's tour. His place felt more like home. Having my own space was a breath of fresh air after Andre's place. Not that I wasn't grateful, but having an actual room with a door that closed was pure luxury.

Just as I was settling into a daily routine, I got called to go back out for another two-month stretch with LFO. This time, it was smaller club dates. Getting back out on the road gave me a deeper understanding of performing and picking up choreography on the fly. By the time I returned to L.A., in the summer of 2000, I felt like I was improving. But the hustle of auditions hit me hard. I wasn't quite making it to the final cuts for big gigs, but I was getting closer.

I could feel the momentum building.

I asked my agent, Brendan, to list the top choreographers working in the industry, so I could figure out who was consistently booking jobs and learn their styles. I began taking classes more strategically, focusing on those same choreographers and analyzing how they moved. Around that time, I booked a small music video gig for one of Rodney Jerkins's artists. It wasn't a big payday, maybe $250 a day, but it kept me working.

Then, out of nowhere, I got a call from Brendan: I'd been booked for Pink's world tour.

The craziest part? I didn't even audition.

Eddie Morales, one of Pink's dancers/choreographers, and now one of my best friends, had hired me. One of their dancers was leaving for another gig, and Eddie had seen tape of me somewhere—maybe a class, maybe a show. To this day, I still don't know exactly how he found me. But what mattered was that I got the job.

I loved Pink's music. This was her first album when she was still doing R&B. Tracks like *Most Girls* and *There You Go* were massive. Being handpicked without auditioning was mind-blowing. Two days after wrapping the music video, I was in rehearsals for a worldwide tour.

Pink's tour was special. Performing on the world stage was only part of it—it was the people who made it unforgettable. Eddie, Marty Kudelka (who was Janet Jackson's choreographer at the time and would later become Justin Timberlake's), and I became a tight-knit crew. Everything just clicked, the choreography, the chemistry, the vibe.

We worked hard and had fun. Smoking weed, gambling on NBA 2K on the Dreamcast, and hanging on the bus for hours. Pink was different. She was young, but grounded, no-BS, all business. Most of the time anyway. While we partied, she stayed disciplined, focusing on her craft, taking care of herself. She felt like one of us, but she had this undeniable star power. I mean here was this girl younger than me who had it all figured out, and I was just starting to put the pieces together in my life. Watching her navigate her rise to fame was inspirational.

This tour gave me so many firsts. My first time traveling internationally, performing outside the U.S., seeing the world. The Australia leg was like stepping onto another planet. I grew up watching *National Geographic* and always dreamed of going there. It was toward the end of the tour, and we were all jacked to get there. We had a three-week stretch lined up down under, and the vibe was high. We'd been performing for months together by now and had it down to a science. Before we left, we all met at Millennium Dance Complex in L.A., where the buses would pick us up to shuttle us to LAX. Everyone was doing their last-minute checks, and Pink's tour manager, Mark Singletary, a massive, intimidating guy with a military background, laid down the law.

"Empty your bags. Make sure you don't have anything stupid on you," he said, his deep voice booming through the studio. "Australia doesn't mess around. Don't be the one who gets us all in trouble."

We all laughed it off, but I took him seriously. I emptied my bags, triple-checked everything, then packed carefully for the trip. The flight to Sydney was brutal. I've never been a fan of flying, and the thought of spending fifteen hours over the ocean had my anxiety pumping through the roof. My ritual was simple: drink until I could sleep, or at least pretend to. By the time we landed, I'd probably knocked back a dozen rum and cokes. I was a wreck.

When we finally got off the plane in Sydney, I could barely stand. Mark, the tour manager, took one look at me and asked, "Are you okay?" I mumbled something about having one too many drinks and tried to pull myself together. But as we headed toward customs, I knew I wasn't fooling anyone.

Walking through customs felt like being funneled through a gauntlet. You either got a straightforward pass-through or a detour into a high-security inspection area. Of course, they pulled me aside. I was green in the face, reeking of alcohol, and clearly out of sorts. A customs agent directed me to a counter, where she ordered me to empty my backpack.

As I dumped everything out, my stomach dropped.

A gram of weed tumbled out onto the counter.

There is fear, and then there's shitting yourself in pure terror. I slapped my hand over the weed and leaned up against the counter, like I was just casually steadying myself. The agent asked if I was okay, and I stammered, "Yeah, I just don't fly well. Had a couple of drinks." I forced a weak smile, trying to sell it.

She nodded and started rummaging through my stuff. As soon as she looked away, I fucking slid the gram off the counter, onto the floor, and nudged it with my foot under the table. I was sweating bullets. There were cops and immigration agents everywhere. All I could think was: *I'm going to jail. I'm going to get fired. I'm fucked.*

The agent swabbed my bag for explosives. When I saw stems and bits of weed attached to the swab, I thought I was done for. But to my shock, the test came back clean, and she gave me the all-clear. I packed my stuff up as fast as I could, trying not to shake as I slipped my lighter out of my pocket, and "accidentally" dropped it on the ground so that it made a loud enough noise to be heard. Whoops. Then I bent down, grabbed the lighter, grabbed the gram, stuffed everything in my pocket in one smooth motion, and took off. As soon as I was outside, I tossed the weed in the nearest trash can. When I rejoined the group, Mark was livid. I apologized, knowing I'd dodged a bullet.

After a short flight from Sydney, we landed in Melbourne.

I was still hungover, barely able to function.

As we arrived at the hotel, Pink greeted us with a surprise.

"You've got 45 minutes," she said. "Shower, change, and meet me at the bar."

I dragged myself upstairs and spent most of those 45 minutes lying on the shower floor, trying to pull myself together. When I made it back down, Pink had lined up ten shots of Jaeger at the bar. "Drink," she said.

We each took two shots and piled into a van. After a two-hour drive into the middle of nowhere, we arrived at a ranch. Pink had arranged a full-day horseback safari for us. We spent hours riding through the jungle, taking in the breathtaking wildlife and scenery. It was unreal, straight out of the *National Geographic* specials I used to watch as a kid. We saw black cockatoos (which I didn't even know existed), huge monitor lizards, koalas, kangaroos, and more. By the end of it, after kicking my hangover, I felt like a new person. The safari was one of the most incredible experiences of my life. Not for Eddie, though. Eddie found out about an hour or two into the jungle that he was allergic to horses. Little by little, he started to itch. Halfway through the ride, we had to stop because his face was swelling up. You see, Eddie was from Brooklyn, N.Y., the only horse he'd ever seen were the kind cops rode for crowd control. This was his first time riding one. All of us were pretty concerned for him, but there was only one way out. He had to sit on that horse the entire ride before getting any meds. By the time we got back, his face looked like a chipmunk. Marty and I were dying laughing at him once we realized he was going to be okay.

Our shows generated a massive amount of attention. At every stop, other dancers and artists would watch from the side of the stage. Even at radio-sponsored festivals with dozens of acts performing, our set stood out. We didn't have flashy props or elaborate staging. It was all about raw talent, energy, and connection with the audience. The industry took notice. By the end of the tour in early 2001, I knew I had grown immensely as a dancer and performer. That was the moment I realized I could thrive in the music industry. The connections, lessons, and experiences from that tour laid the foundation for everything to follow. Pink's leadership and down-to-earth vibe kept us grounded. She made sure we worked hard, but also that we enjoyed the ride. That tour was a pivotal chapter in my life, one that solidified my love for dance and gave me the confidence to keep pushing forward.

Touring with Pink proved to be a gateway. The experience opened countless doors for me in ways I could have never imagined. So many iconic choreographers and dancers were involved in that project, it was like a creative melting pot that drew everyone's attention in the dance community. Over those eight months, we showcased something special. By the time I returned to L.A., I was operating at a whole new level, walking into auditions with confidence, consistently making it to the final rounds, and eventually getting booked without even having to audition.

At the heart of this momentum was the rapport I had built with choreographers, dancers, and agents in the community. They began to see me as someone solid, someone dependable. During that time, my relationship with my best friend Jimmy also evolved. Watching Jimmy thrive sparked a competitive fire in me. I don't know if Jimmy ever saw it that way, but by the time I returned from Pink's tour, I felt like I had stepped out of his shadow. The friendly rivalry had pushed me to grow into the best version of myself as a dancer. And now, I wasn't just competing—I was eating.

In the entertainment industry, good work gets you more work. That was the reality I was living. Choreographers I worked with knew I would show up, get the job done, and be easy to work with. Word spread. On the heels of the Pink tour, my career expanded into music videos, TV shows, commercials, and award shows. I danced in Destiny's Child's *Survivor* music video and performed with them at the Grammys and Soul Train Awards. I landed gigs on *The Drew Carey Show*, and even did a Target commercial in Toronto.

None of it felt like work. I was doing something I loved and making good money doing it. Every gig felt like a stepping stone, a new adventure. For a kid from Fresno, this was my NBA or NFL, a dream come true.

I remember once taking my mom to a Janet Jackson concert in Fresno. I was nineteen. We were in the nosebleeds with binoculars, and I told her, "That's going to be me one day. I'm going to be right there on that stage." She just smiled and said, "Yeah right! Okay, Kevin." A few years later, I was living in L.A., dancing for major artists and making more money than my parents ever expected. My mom never let me forget how I'd spoken it into existence.

By 2001, my career had hit its stride. I'd worked with Aaliyah, Ginuwine, Destiny's Child, Pink, No Doubt, and many others. Everything was working out. For years, Jimmy and I had hoped to get out on the road together, and when we finally both booked Christina Milian's world tour, we were so hyped.

But life had other plans.

Weeks before rehearsals, I auditioned for Michael Jackson's *You Rock My World* music video. The process was intense, and for the last spot it came down to me and my boy Marty Kudelka, who was Janet Jackson's choreographer. When neither of us got a callback, I assumed the job was canceled. A week into Christina Milian's rehearsals, I got a call from Flii, one of Michael's choreographers. He told me to clean up and meet him at the Universal Studios backlot immediately.

I had no idea what was waiting for me.

When I arrived, the massive sound stage was nearly empty, just a row of mirrors, a sound system, and the four choreographers working for MJ at the time. Richmond and Tone Talauega,

Samoan brothers who'd been with MJ since they were teenagers; Flii, who was a choreographer for Usher and a friend of mine; and Micheal Rooney, who hired me for the Target commercial. The crew handed me a release form to sign and then told me I was about to hear the track. They wanted me to freestyle. The pressure was unreal. They played *You Rock My World*, and I did my thing. I left not knowing if I'd nailed it or blown it. A few hours later, my phone rang. I had booked the job. The excitement was overwhelming, but it came with a heavy choice. I was thrilled to work with Michael Jackson, but it meant giving up the Christina Milian tour, and a chance to tour the world with Jimmy and make good money doing it. It was an easy choice to make, though: working with MJ was a once in a lifetime opportunity. I went back to Christina's rehearsals the next day and broke the news. They were disappointed, but they understood. I knew this was a chance to be part of something with a true icon and legend. What we didn't know at the time was that this would be Michael's last album.

Walking into rehearsals felt surreal. I had been on major world tours, but this was like starting from square one. I was so nervous, it felt like my first gig all over again. Because as a dancer, as a performer, this was the biggest stage you could ever stand on. The whole video had this Cuban *Smooth Criminal* vibe, like he never fully got out of that phase. But it's Michael. He could do whatever the hell he wanted when it came to his craft. For the first week and a half, he didn't even show up to rehearsals. We just drilled the choreography over and over and over until we had it down. Then one day, the energy in the room shifted. The air grew still. Everyone went quiet. You could feel Michael's presence before he even stepped foot into the room. A very surreal feeling.

Wearing sunglasses and moving with an almost ethereal grace, he waved at us, set a chair in front of the mirrors, sat down, and said, "Run it."

We started dancing.

He stopped us almost immediately and said, "No music. Run it with the click track." I didn't understand why until later. Michael didn't just see the dance; he felt it. With the click track, he could hear everything, the rhythm, the timing, and even the tiniest misstep. So we start again, he's sitting in the chair, sunglasses on, but you could still see he had his eyes closed.

And I was off. By one beat.

This motherfucker opens his eyes and looks right at me.

He could tell that it was me who was off even with his eyes closed. He knew exactly where it came from, exactly who it was. My stomach hit my throat. I felt exposed.

Then he stops everything and says, "Alright, let's run it again. Calm down."

That was it. He knew. He knew it was my first time working with him, knew I was nervous. He wasn't mad. Just precise. Michael didn't chase perfection for the sake of it. Every detail was a way to connect, make the audience feel something real.

Michael shot the video like a movie.

We had two weeks of rehearsals, and then eight days of actual shooting. He was meticulous to a fault, but also playful and charismatic. Michael and his choreographers taught me to view dance as more than just movement. For him, dance was an emotion, a form of expression that transcended words. He instilled that perspective in all of us. Dancing behind him meant more than hitting the steps—it was about connecting with the music, and tapping into something bigger than all of us. Something that when seen or practiced can move people to their core. To me, this was his magic. Being able to tap into something spiritually unexplainable. The same way ancient tribes would dance around a bonfire connecting to a different level of consciousness. Michael learned how to do this at will and was absolutely surgical with it. It was his superpower—the reason he stood out above all the rest.

Of course, this was all before all the allegations against him came out. But at the time, as a young dancer trying to make it, the experience was another sign that I was right where I was meant to be.

CHAPTER THREE

By July 2002, I was in a relationship with Shar Jackson. Shar was an actress, best known for playing Niecy in the hit TV series *Moesha*. I first met her briefly at a party in Vegas, but we only really connected later in L.A., exchanging numbers after bumping into each other at a dance class. Eventually, we began seeing each other.

At the time, Shar would often stay with me at my place. She lived in Orange County, but spent weeks at a time with me in Los Angeles. She had two kids from a previous relationship, Cassie and Donnie, who were about five and seven at the time, and her mom helped take care of them. We were inseparable for a while. It was young love; and at that moment, it seemed like everything was falling into place.

Then, before our first daughter was born, Shar had a miscarriage. That loss hit me hard, more than I realized at the time. I felt ready to have a child. I'd always talked about wanting a big family, even as a kid. By the time I hit my teenage years, that dream had taken a backseat to chasing girls and figuring out life; but deep down, I still wanted it. After the miscarriage, I think I was just ready to try again. I loved Shar deeply, and I was financially stable enough to support a family.

Or so I thought.

No one can truly prepare you for fatherhood; nothing matches the moment you first hold your child. The first time I cradled my daughter in my arms and saw her eyes open—it was overwhelming. That moment is imprinted in my mind. Instantly, everything changed. My priorities shifted forever.

Shar and I were together until our daughter, Kori, was about two years old. During that period, my dance career remained strong. I booked *You Got Served*, a dance movie featuring Steve Harvey, Omarion, and others. Around the same time, my boy Marty got a call to choreograph for the last leg of NSYNC's tour. This was just before the drama involving Britney, Justin Timberlake, and Wade Robson exploded publicly.

Wade had been close with Justin, but after the rumors about Britney and Wade surfaced, Justin and the group parted ways with him. That's when Marty stepped into a permanent position. Justin was gearing up to transition from NSYNC to his solo career, and Marty became instrumental in choreographing for Justin. Marty hired me for Justin's *Like I Love You* music video and the VMAs. Justin's first solo tour was on the table; but by then, I couldn't. I couldn't leave my daughter. Even traveling for gigs like the VMAs, I'd catch late flights home that same night to be with her. That's when I realized touring was no longer a viable option.

Shar and I had our ups and downs. If we were both working, things were great; but when work slowed down, it got tough. There were moments when bills went unpaid, and the lights got turned off. I booked *You Got Served* during one of those tougher times. It was an amazing opportunity and a great lifeline.

After Kori was born, we moved to Orange County. I left the shared apartment in Sherman Oaks where I'd been living with Jimmy and Eddie. Marty had been living in the apartment above us. They all moved into a new spot near Whitsett, close to the little par-three golf course behind Jerry's Deli in Studio City. Meanwhile, I moved to Yorba Linda with Shar and our daughter. It was a beautiful area, but the commute to L.A. for work was brutal. During *You Got Served*, I drove daily from Yorba Linda to L.A. for early 7:30 a.m. calls, often two and a half hours each way.

After *You Got Served*, I booked a gig with Usher for one of the award shows. The jobs were coming in, but I knew I couldn't keep up the same pace. My priorities had shifted, and my daughter came first. Touring was off the table. Life was different now, and I was figuring out how to make it all work. I was young. I think when you're in your early twenties, you don't really know someone, even after six months or a year. You don't really know yourself, for that matter. It takes time, longer than you think, to really understand a person. It wasn't that Shar was a bad person.

We just didn't mesh the way I thought we would. In hindsight, much of that was on me, not being mature or prepared enough to handle everything.

The one thing that was clear to me, though, was my daughter. There was no way in hell I was ever going to leave her. At that time, I was all-in as a parent, determined to give her the best life possible. But I also found myself feeling the pull to get away. I was navigating this new life that came with Shar already having two kids from a previous relationship, and that wasn't the hard part. The hard part was that it wasn't just us. We had a full house: her mom, her siblings, and her brother's girlfriend all moved in with us. Don't get me wrong, I loved them all; they are great people, and I appreciate them and everything they did. But I was twenty-four, and I just wasn't ready for that kind of dynamic.

On top of that, little things began to wear on me. Like, when we'd go to events, Shar wouldn't walk the red carpet with me. She would have me wait on the other side for her, avoiding the cameras. At first, I didn't think much of it. But as our relationship became serious, and especially after we had Kori, it bothered me. She wanted to keep her private life private, which I understood. It was part of her work, part of who she was. But there was also the layer of us being a mixed-race couple. She would talk about how people might frown upon it in certain circles. At the time, I was naïve about all that; and honestly, I probably didn't handle it as well as I could have. I didn't have the experience or the emotional tools to handle it well.

I think now that a lot of it came down to the fact that I've always been searching for that one person. Each relationship I've had taught me something about myself and what I truly needed in a partner. It's been a process, a messy, sometimes painful process, but one that's helped me grow.

With Shar, it wasn't like we had these explosive fights or major drama. She was super chill, and I think we both tried to make it work. But sometimes, it's just not a fit. It's not anyone's fault. It's just life. We were trying to force something that wasn't meant to be. We could be great co-parents, but as partners, it just wasn't there.

I think part of the reason things dragged on longer than they should have was because I've always been a passive person. I avoid confrontation whenever I can. I try to be mindful of other people's feelings; and because of that, I've stayed in relationships longer than I probably should have. That was definitely the case with Shar. I didn't want to hurt her, but deep down I knew we weren't right for each other.

Things with Shar had been unraveling for some time. I didn't know for sure that it was over, but I felt it heading in that direction. I was spending more time away, crashing back at Eddie and Jimmy's place. Part of me was looking for my next big gig, trying to support my family. But part of me was also looking for an escape.

Shar had no desire to go out. She rarely went out socially; when she did, it was mostly for work events or Hollywood functions. I wanted to go out, have fun, and forget about the pressures of life. So, I found ways to do that on my own.

It wasn't like I hated being home. I loved being around my daughter, and Shar's family was great. But it could get overwhelming, always having so many people around, so much going on. It wasn't my direct family, so it was easier to detach, to step away. I'd head to Vegas for a couple of nights or go up to stay with the boys just to breathe. It wasn't like I was gone for weeks, but it was enough.

I wasn't just looking for work anymore. I was looking for a way out.

Then we found out Shar was pregnant again, adding even more weight to an already difficult situation. It was a lot to process. I was already feeling the strain in our relationship and trying to figure out my next steps. I didn't know how to balance my family, career, and need for space. At the same time, I was torn. I was genuinely happy and excited to welcome another child, but couldn't ignore the fact that my feelings toward Shar were changing. I kept telling myself that if I just held on for the kids, maybe things would work out.

Ultimately, I realized forcing it wasn't working. It wasn't fair to Shar, to our kids, or to myself. I've always been a family-oriented person. I grew up in a big, blended family, so the idea of family has always been important to me. But I also knew that staying in a relationship just for the sake of the kids wasn't the right move.

In my twenties, I lived a full life—experienced the world, partied hard, and met incredible people. But even then, it wasn't just about the chase or the thrill. Every relationship, every connection, was teaching me something, preparing me for what I have now. It was all part of the journey to find the right person, the right fit.

My chapter with Shar didn't end as expected, but I'm grateful for its lessons. I'm grateful for the family we created. The way things ended with her forced me to confront some tough truths.

CHAPTER FOUR

The story of Britney and me began on a Monday night at Joseph's, a Hollywood nightclub that was *the* spot, packed with industry types, dancers, and the kind of people you'd never expect to cross paths with anywhere else on the planet. That night, I was with the crew: Big Mike, Big Rob, and a few others, hanging at Jimmy and Eddie's before we all headed out. As we got ready to go, Big Rob mentioned that Britney was gonna be there that night.

It didn't hit me as a big deal at first. I had been around a lot of celebrities and wasn't some star-struck kid. I was twenty-five, feeling myself, and used to that world. I'd met her briefly before on the LFO tour—a quick, casual intro, no big deal. I looked at the guys, half-joking but kind of serious, and said, "I'm gonna see what's up with her tonight." They laughed it off like—*yeah, sure, okay, buddy.*

Fast forward, we're at Joseph's. It was packed, that usual early 2000s vibe: hip-hop blasting, wall-to-wall people, barely room to move, let alone dance. But that was my scene. I was having a good time, dancing with a few of Britney's dancers, including Theresa, who I already knew from back in the day. I wasn't trying to be obvious, but I couldn't help sneaking glances at Britney. And I could tell she noticed.

She called Theresa over, whispered something in her ear, and the next thing I know Theresa's dragging me over to her booth, shooting me a look as if to say: *you better not mess this up.* Britney was sitting with her assistant and some other dancers. But the moment I sat down, everything else kind of just faded into the background. It was just me and her.

Britney had this presence about her. She was confident but not intimidating, engaging without trying too hard. We talked for a little while and then hit the dance floor. Nothing too wild, just a little playful back-and-forth. Honestly, at the time, in my twenty-five year old mind, I was just thinking about smashing that. But she had this way of making you feel at ease, like you didn't have to put on a front, or keep your guard up. I felt like I could be myself.

Eventually, we made our way back to the booth. By then, the night was winding down. Britney leaned in close, her voice low enough that I had to tilt my head to hear her. "We're heading back to the hotel for a swim. You coming?"

"Yeah, I'm down."

We piled into an SUV. Britney, a couple of her dancers, and me. By the time we got to the Beverly Hills Hotel, the adrenaline from the club was wearing off. She had a bungalow with a private pool and hot tub. Everyone jumped into the water in their underwear. Britney got into the hot tub. I rolled up my pants and sat on the edge next to her with my feet in the water.

At one point, she noticed the tattoo on my arm, the one for my daughter, Kori. She reached out, tracing it lightly with her fingers.

"What's this mean?" she asked, her voice quiet.

"It's for my daughter," I said. "Her sign, her birthday."

I could tell she was surprised, like she wasn't expecting that. Not in a bad way, just caught off guard. Like now she saw something in me that didn't quite fit the image she had in her head.

"Oh," she said softly.

"Does that upset you?" I asked, not sure what to make of her reaction.

"No, not at all," she said. "That's cool."

Everyone was bouncing back and forth from the pool to the hot tub, but we stayed where we were. Her brother Bryan was there, hanging out for a while. Then, while everyone was still swimming, Britney got out of the hot tub, grabbed my arm, and led me into the bungalow. Everyone else must have got the message and eventually left. I wasn't worried about anyone else though.

As soon as we got into the bungalow, Britney turned around, slipped off her underwear and started kissing me, tearing at my clothes with both hands. We stumbled toward the bed while I struggled to kick my pants off my ankles. This. Is. Happening.

Okay. Sorry, calm down, that's as detailed as I'm going to get on that.

What happened between us that night was purely physical. It felt like we were feeding off each other's energy, caught in this whirlwind of chemistry and connection. Very passionate, very intense. In my mind, I was fine with it just being a fling. But, obviously, it didn't turn out that way.

What started as one night became two, then stretched into three, the whole time holed up in that bungalow. We talked, getting to know each other. She opened up, telling me about her life, her struggles, the things she'd been through.

For me, it was interesting, unexpected. I thought this would be a one night stand, and then it would be done. But it became more than that. We became really close and connected over those first few days. I realized a lot of the things Britney cared about, who she was beyond the spotlight, were exactly what drew me in so fast. Someone independent, with her own life, her own strength. She was her own person, confident. That was a big deal for me. From the beginning, Britney beat to her own drum; she did what she wanted to do, when she wanted to do it, and that was a huge turn-on.

When we finally left the bungalow, I had no idea what was coming. She was tired of being cooped up in the hotel and wanted to get out. She loved driving her SL550 with the top down, and I just went along with it, never thinking about the attention it would draw. From the moment we pulled out of the Beverly Hills Hotel, it turned into a full-blown parade of paparazzi. What started off as ten cars of press tripled as we kept driving. She showed me her old house in the Hollywood Hills, and then we cut through the canyons, eventually heading toward Sunset Beach, right off the Pacific Coast Highway. I didn't know it then, but this day would set the tone for everything that followed.

It all felt surreal. I hadn't even had a chance to go home and change since the night we met, so there I was, in a baseball hat, white tee shirt, jeans, and my Air Force Ones. The moment we stepped out of the car, the paparazzi swarmed us. It was overwhelming. They snapped photos and shouted questions. They completely surrounded us. But she handled it like a pro— cool, calm. She asked them to give us some space after a few photos, and surprisingly, they listened. They backed off to their cars, giving us a moment to ourselves.

We stayed on the beach, just sitting near the waves, smoking and talking. I can't remember all the details of our conversation, something about how she managed this kind of attention every day. She shrugged it off like it was normal, but it was clear she didn't love it. Something shifted in her demeanor the moment the paparazzi showed up. Not standoffish with me, just…more anxious. Her whole energy changed. She'd been dealing with it since she was sixteen. For me, though, it was all new, and it was insane. I decided to give her a piggyback ride out to the water to give us some space. And even then, I couldn't shake the feeling of being watched. The paparazzi stayed parked, waiting for any new angle to capture.

Those first few weeks were a whirlwind, an emotional and sensory overload that I couldn't have prepared for if I tried. I remember calling my mom early on, trying to explain everything. Her response, though well-meaning, was rooted in disbelief. She thought I was calling about some one-night stand, that this whole thing would blow over. But I had to spell it out for her: "No, Mom, you don't understand. This is going to be everywhere." And I meant everywhere. The intensity was unreal—twenty, thirty paparazzi cars tailing us all over the map. This was much more than a one-night stand or simple fling. This was a massive, life-altering change in existence.

Before this, life wasn't exactly quiet. Working in the entertainment industry already meant living in a fast-paced world, but this was a different beast. It felt like jumping into a race car without a seatbelt at the Daytona 500, the whole world watching. The attention, the emotions, the sheer mayhem of it all—it was like stepping into an alternate universe, watching the wormhole close behind you, and there was no going back.

Then there was the public perception, how the world saw me. That was a trip. I knew what people thought. They looked at me like, *Oh man, this dude jumped out of his trailer and into Britney's mansion.* That's exactly how it must have looked to a hell of a lot of people. And they weren't entirely wrong. Britney and I came from completely different worlds. I was not famous, nobody knew who I was. Britney was loved by everyone and her fans probably wanted to see her with someone they viewed was equal to her status.

As much as I loved being with her, part of me was terrified. What had I gotten myself into? I was a young guy living in the moment, but this was unlike anything I'd ever experienced. It wasn't just our private concern. The whole world was watching. Tabloid press, paparazzi shadowing our every move, twenty-four seven. This was a San Andreas-level seismic shift in my reality. And in the madness of it all, I'd barely stopped to process what was happening. That first week set the stage for everything that followed. It was just the first loop on the rollercoaster ride that would define not only my career, but my identity. In ways that I'm still coming to terms with today.

We had spent days together before I even went back to my apartment to grab clothes. Even then, she was already making calls to her team, telling them in no uncertain terms that she would not go to Europe without me. "This tour isn't happening unless he comes with me," she said. And she meant it. She skipped her flight and refused to budge until the details were worked out. Her insistence was overwhelming. I remember thinking: *Wow, this is a lot of pressure*. But at the same time, I felt like I couldn't say no. We felt like we owed it to ourselves to see where this goes.

Going on tour with her was a big decision. And it came with consequences. Leaving my daughter—for one. Knowing I wouldn't see her for weeks. I'd been splitting time between Los Angeles and Orange County for months, staying close to Kori, avoiding tours, staying off the road. But now I was committing to being away longer than ever before. As if things weren't already crazy—the Britney situation, the press, all that emotional turbulence...

It was a bumpy ride, to say the least.

For all of us.

I handled the breakup with Shar poorly. I wasn't honest or direct. Before I left for Europe to meet up with Britney, I saw her and Kori. I told her that I'd booked a commercial shooting overseas. I knew it would hurt her, and I didn't want that. If I could go back in time, I'd handle that whole thing differently. But life doesn't work like that. We fuck up and we learn.

When I finally called her, I remember pacing the floor, heart pounding. I told her about Britney, about the connection we had, and how I couldn't ignore it. I could hear the heartbreak in her voice, and the pain it caused. She was angry. But under the anger was something deeper, a sadness I couldn't undo.

I tried to reassure her about our kids, that I wasn't walking away from them. No matter what happened between us, they would always come first. My parents set that example for me when they split, showing me how to hold it together for your children. I lived by that. I paid child support consistently, without court or fights. I went above and beyond because I wanted to. Even when money got tight, I still made sure they had what they needed.

But none of that changed the fact that I failed her.

I should've been more upfront about how unhappy I'd become. I let things unravel instead of facing them head-on. I told myself the distance would make things easier, but it just delayed the inevitable. By the time we spoke, it was too late. I had already let her piece together the truth on her own. The photos of Britney and me on the beach helped.

Writing this book has forced me to confront things I tried to bury. And how I left Shar—that was one of the hardest. I just want Kori and Kaleb to know:

I wasn't the man I needed to be.

I wasn't the man I *wanted* to be.

And for that, I am truly sorry.

CHAPTER FIVE

W hen I joined Britney's tour, I didn't feel the need to prove myself to the people around her. By that point in my life, I had already been on a few tours. It felt natural, like slipping back into something familiar. Tour life has its own vibe; a unique rhythm where everyone quickly bonds into one big family, almost like a traveling circus. Sure, I'm certain people around her were questioning me at first, wondering who I was or what my intentions might be, but that didn't faze me. I wasn't worried about earning their approval. My focus was completely on her, our relationship, and making sure she felt loved and supported.

Her assistant, Felicia—"Fee"—was amazing right from the beginning. Fee was one of those people who radiates positivity. She had that classic southern charm, the kind that lights up a room, even under pressure. She always checked in with me, asked if I was okay, if I needed anything, and made sure I felt comfortable. She didn't have to go out of her way for me, but she did, and that kindness meant something.

The rest of her team welcomed me in their own time. I never felt like anyone was giving me the side-eye or looking at me like I didn't belong. No one made me feel uncomfortable or out of place. The atmosphere was warm, and while I'm sure there may have been questions behind closed doors, I never felt judged.

Being thrust into the limelight was wild, an emotional and logistical whirlwind. Through all the madness that came our way, I tried to stay grounded, especially with her, and not let all the external noise influence the way I felt. It was important to me to keep things real because that's who I am and that's what I felt she needed. She'd spent so much of her life surrounded by people who wanted something from her. But I wanted her to know I wasn't one of them. I wasn't there for the fame or attention. I was there for her. What anyone else thought didn't matter to me.

The tour itself was like stepping into another world. We traveled from city to city, and when she wasn't performing, we were inseparable. She let her guard down with me in ways I don't think she had with many people. She could be herself, open up, really confide in me. We were building trust. Everything was so fresh, but it felt so right.

I remember the first show I flew into on the European leg—it might've been at the O2 Arena—and everything was still brand new. I was backstage, soaking it all in, when I spotted Lonnie.

And man, seeing him in that moment hit different. We hadn't talked in a while, but the history was there.

I met Lonnie through Shar, back when I was still with her. He wasn't her personal security or anything, just a solid dude she knew from the set of *Moesha*. He was doing security work there. Lonnie had even come by to meet Kori when she was just a baby, so yeah, he was more than just some guy I bumped into. We weren't best friends or talking every day, but there was respect there. Family-adjacent.

Lonnie's this big, intimidating presence. You see him and think he could level a room. But truth is, he's a giant teddy bear. A deacon turned pastor. The type of man who'd lay his life down for someone he loves, and in the same breath, pray for your healing. Later on, I actually hired him to do security for the boys. That's how much I trusted him.

Anyway, that night backstage, Lonnie walked straight up to me, and in classic Lonnie fashion, pulled me aside with a "Yo, can I talk to you for a minute?" I knew it was coming. He'd definitely heard the noise—me leaving Shar, jumping into this thing with Britney. He looked me dead in the eye and hit me with, "What are you doing?" No fluff. No small talk.

And I just told him the truth. I was unhappy. Things were falling apart with Shar. I met Britney, we connected, and I was trying to see where it would go. Lonnie didn't judge. That's not who he is. But he said, "Be careful." And he meant it. He knew I wasn't some player or clout chaser, but he was close with Shar, so of course there were emotions there. That moment stuck with me.

Then came Q, another guy from Britney's old security team I knew from the scene. He'd done work with Britney back in the day, when she was just starting out. Him and Big Rob were her guys from the time she was, like, sixteen, up to her early twenties. They'd seen it all. Q wasn't one to sugarcoat anything either. He rolled up mid-convo, looked at me, and straight up said, "You're on a sinking ship. What the fuck are you doing?"

We weren't strangers either. Q was dating my friend, Angela, so I'd known him for a while. We all ran in the same Hollywood circles. But that night, his energy was different. Real. Protective.

I didn't listen. I wasn't about to let someone else's experiences shape mine. I told Q the same thing I told Lonnie. I had to see this through. I was already catching real feelings for Britney, and no warning or side-eyes were gonna change that. I don't judge people by their past. I judge them by how they treat me, in the moment, right now.

Now that I think about it, that night in Europe was the first real warning. Not just people talking behind closed doors, but face-to-face confrontations from people who had been there, seen shit, and didn't want me walking into the same fire. But I was already in it. And I wasn't ready to walk away.

Then came Amsterdam.

It was supposed to be unforgettable—iconic city, vibrant nightlife, and the kind of freedom you can't find anywhere else.

But for me, it became unforgettable for other reasons. The night started out simple enough. We all went out: me, Britney, and some of the dancers and staff from the tour, including Theresa, the girl who introduced us at Joseph's. It was one of those loose, carefree evenings where everyone was dancing, drinking, and just having a good time.

We stayed out late, hitting one of the city's nightclubs until at least one or two in the morning. It felt like just another fun time on tour—a night you laugh about later. When we got back to the hotel, the group piled out of the SUV and headed inside. Britney and I went to our room, but shortly after, she said she'd be right back.

At first, I didn't think much of it. The hotel floor was ours; they had booked it out for the entire tour, so everyone's rooms were nearby. But as time passed, I began to wonder what was taking so long. I was thinking maybe she was catching up with someone or handling something tour-related.

Eventually, I decided to check if everything was okay. I stepped into the hallway, our door still cracked, like most on the floor, and headed toward the elevators. As I passed one of the rooms, I glanced inside—and froze. There she was. Theresa was sitting on the edge of the bed. Britney stood between her legs, hands on her face, and they were fucking going at it. Full-on making out. It was one of those moments that hits you so fast, your brain can't even begin to process it. You just stand there, stunned, not sure what's real.

I didn't say a word. Just stood there, watching. For a second, nobody moved. Then they both looked up and saw me, and I turned and walked away. My heart was racing, but not with excitement. It was something colder, a sudden clarity.

This wasn't what I signed up for. So I got the hell out of there. As soon as I got back to our room, I grabbed my suitcase and started packing. At that point, I cared about nothing else—I just wanted out.

I picked up the phone, called Fee, and asked her to book me the first flight back to the States. I didn't care what time it was. I was ready to sit at the airport all night if necessary.

I was done.

As I finished packing, Britney came back into the room. She knew immediately, just by looking at me, that something was wrong.

"What's going on?" she demanded, her voice laced with panic.

"I'm leaving," I told her, my tone cold and final. "You can do whatever you want, but this isn't what I came here for. If this is how it's gonna be, I'm out."

In an instant, her expression shifted from confusion to regret. She started apologizing, explaining, promising it would never happen again. She told me she didn't realize how serious I was about us, that she was overwhelmed, and it had been a mistake. For a moment, I saw her vulnerability. She was desperate for me to stay. Begging me.

I could tell she meant it. But I was still furious. Still hurt. I told her that I wasn't there for the "extra shit," as I called it. I wasn't interested in a relationship that involved more than two people. I wasn't judging her. I was simply laying down boundaries. I wasn't going to let this set the tone for whatever we were building. Not to mention that Theresa was Marty's ex-girlfriend.

I didn't think about it then, but that moment was a turning point for both of us. It was our first fight, or whatever you want to call it. I think it was the moment she realized I wasn't there for the fame or the perks. I was only there for her. The fact that I was ready to walk away, even after everything I had already given up to be with her, proved it was real.

In the days that followed, something seemed to change between us. She became more intentional, more thoughtful about how we were together. It felt like we were truly starting to figure out what we meant to each other. Still, there were lingering doubts. I couldn't shake the nagging voice in my head that wondered if I had made the right choice. I was thousands of miles away from my daughter. And the life I had stepped into wasn't just fast-paced—it was relentless. Every city brought new challenges. New eyes watching us, waiting for us to falter. Her fame wasn't just hers anymore; it enveloped me too—and at times, it was suffocating.

There were also flashes of intense joy. I remember one afternoon in Sweden, sneaking away to a park near the hotel. We lay in the grass, made out, and talked about everything and nothing. Of course, photos of that afternoon surfaced later; but for those few hours, it was just us. Small, seemingly insignificant times like that became the foundation of our connection. They reminded me why I was there, making the madness seem suddenly manageable.

More than anything, that tour opened my eyes to her world. I saw firsthand the pressures she faced, the endless demands of the industry, the constant scrutiny. When she had a few glasses of wine, she would open up and vent her frustrations—with the industry, with her team, with the weight of her fame. It was eye-opening, and honestly a little intimidating, to hear just how much she carried every day. Trust didn't come easily to her, and I wanted to be someone she could rely on.

Those weeks in Europe, navigating that emotional minefield together, laid the foundation of our relationship. They tested us, changed us, and ultimately brought us closer together. It was during this time that I began to realize the depth of my feelings. And while the road ahead was anything but certain, I knew one thing for sure: I was falling in love with Britney.

CHAPTER SIX

O nce the European leg of the tour wrapped, we headed straight to New York. I remember the flight vividly, because we were halfway over the Atlantic when Britney brought up marriage. There we were, sitting in first class, sipping cocktails, talking about life, and then—*bam*—she was casually, or maybe not so casually, proposing to me. I wasn't sure if she was serious. Was it just the champagne talking? I kind of laughed it off, played it cool, and told her no. Not in a cruel way, just like, *Nah, not happening.* She was a little shocked I turned her down. I joked it off and changed the subject.

When we landed in New York, she had a packed schedule. There was a music video shoot in Queens for one of her singles, featuring Snoop Dogg, from her latest album. It was the first time I'd ever met him and it wouldn't be the last. The shoot was running late, as they always do, and I was just hanging out in the trailer while she was filming a scene out on the basketball court.

Then, suddenly, Britney's security guard, Tony, burst into the trailer, cradling her in his arms. She'd blown out her knee during the routine. I mean, completely wrecked it—ACL, MCL, whatever. She needed immediate surgery. They canceled the remaining U.S. leg of the tour, and we stayed in New York for the operation. She had this incredible condo in the city, and that became our base. We went from the non-stop commotion of touring to total stillness, just the two of us. I became her support system, helping her recover, making sure she had whatever she needed. We had this time together where we could just *be*. No big production, no cameras, no noise. The world slowed down for us. No more bouncing like a pinball between cities. It was just the two of us, holed up in her condo, navigating the quiet moments. It was a strange time, and as the days went by, and the solitude took hold, I thought about what she'd said on the plane. I kept replaying it in my head, wondering if I'd made a mistake brushing it off. By the time she was well enough to think about flying again, I finally worked up the nerve to ask her the question she'd asked me weeks earlier.

There were no elaborate plans, no scripted speeches. We didn't even have a ring. It all started as a simple, heartfelt conversation, a mutual acknowledgment of what we wanted and where we were headed. We were just two people sitting together, deeply in the moment, deciding that this was it—we were getting married.

Until then, everything had been moving at light speed. This didn't feel rushed; it felt like the natural flow of our lives. We were still getting to know each other, and everything felt perfect. No arguments, no second-guessing, just this intense connection. The truth is, those early months were all a honeymoon phase. When you're young and in love, especially in that whirlwind environment, instant gratification becomes second nature. You don't stop to analyze or question; you just ride the wave.

For me, though, there was one thing I couldn't move past without doing. I told her if we were really getting married, I needed to meet her father first. There was no way I could do it otherwise. I hadn't even met him yet. He was in rehab. Jamie, her dad, was going through his own battles, and that added another layer to the situation. But it meant a lot to me to have his approval before we moved forward.

As soon as we got back to L.A., we started looking for a ring. She had a very specific vision in mind: she wanted it to be vintage. One of her assistants reached out to a contact, a jewelry dealer who specialized in that sort of thing and brought a selection of antique diamond rings for her to choose from. The one she chose was dope: a four-and-a-half or five-carat vintage diamond ring. It had that old-world charm she loved, and it became her first engagement ring. Romantic, unique, timeless—it hit exactly the vibe she was after. But as time passed, her taste shifted. The vintage ring, while beautiful, didn't feel right to her anymore, and she decided she wanted something different.

That's when I got her a second engagement ring, which also doubled as her wedding ring. This one was totally different, a sleek, modern design with a six-and-a-half-carat diamond, meticulously cut and outrageously priced. It better matched where we were in life—bigger, bolder, flashier—and it quickly became her favorite.

As for the original vintage ring, it didn't go to waste. Instead of selling it, I had it transformed into something personal. My jeweler, Leor, based in Las Vegas, took the diamond and reworked it into a pinky ring for me. It became a cool, custom piece, one that carried its own sentimental weight. The rings, like our relationship, tell a story. From the simple beginning without a ring to the extravagant pieces that followed, they marked moments in time—love, change, and motion. Our journey together. Everything unfolding faster than either of us could have ever imagined.

Settling back in Los Angeles felt like a reset. We were staying at Britney's apartment in Santa Monica. She was relieved to be off the road and in no rush to record another album or hit the stage again. Instead, she wanted to take a breather, a year or so to herself. She still planned to head into the studio occasionally, but the focus had shifted. For the first time, it felt like life was just about us.

One of the first things I did was bring my daughter, Kori, over to the apartment. She stayed with us for a couple of days, and that experience was unforgettable. Britney was completely taken with her, totally head over heels. I think that time with Kori sparked something in her, maybe even baby fever. She was talking more about wanting kids. Up to that point, it hadn't really been part of the conversation, but now it was clear: she wanted to start a family.

At the same time, she was deep into planning our wedding. She was completely invested in every detail, excited about what was to come. She was ready—like *ready* ready. She wanted the real deal, the big day, everything done the right way. Me? I was just trying to keep up. There I was, planning our nuptials, and thinking: *How the hell did I even get here?* But everything seemed just right, like it was all exactly how it was supposed to be.

Before any of that went down, however, we had this whole other thing to deal with—her dad, Jamie. He had just gotten out of rehab, and the first time I met him, it was…well, exactly what you'd imagine. Meeting your girlfriend's dad for the first time is always nerve-wracking, but this was next-level. She wasn't just my girlfriend anymore. She was already my fiancée. I'd asked her to marry me before ever speaking to him. I wasn't sure how he was going to take that. But I was about to find out.

I could feel him sizing me up, trying to figure out who I was, what my deal was. And I understood why. This is his daughter. You're supposed to look out for her. I respected that. But man, the energy was heavy. Jamie was cool, though. Sober. Clear-eyed. Southern to the core. We hung out for a couple of hours, talked about golf, cooking, and his time in rehab. Somewhere in there, I hit him with the Big Question.

"Sir, is it okay if I marry your daughter?"

I didn't do it for Britney. She honestly couldn't have cared less. She made it clear: with or without his blessing, we were getting married. But for me, as a dad, with a daughter of my own, I had to ask. Jamie said yes. And I could tell he respected the fact that I came to him straight-up, man to man.

Now, her family dynamic?

That's a whole different story. Louisiana roots, a complicated past. There was a lot of love, but also a lot of *stuff*. You could hear it in the way she talked about them. One day, she was all about her mom. The next, she couldn't stand her. Same with her dad, her brother, her sister. There was just so much history there. And I learned pretty quickly: if I was going to be in Britney's life, I'd have to navigate all of that too.

While Britney and I were planning our wedding, my second child with Shar was born.

I remember the morning vividly. I got a phone call from Shar's mom. Shar had gone into labor. She was in Orange County. I was in Santa Monica. I jumped in my car and floored it to the hospital. Shar had a quick labor, so quick that by the time I arrived, Kaleb had already been born. I think I was stepping out of the elevator when I got the news. I missed his birth by maybe a few minutes. When I walked into the room, Shar was holding him. My son was here, and I couldn't hold back the tears. Seeing Kaleb for the first time was incredible, even if the circumstances were a little awkward.

When the nurse took him for some tests, I went up to the roof to get some air. I couldn't go out front—in case the paparazzi were camped outside. I was overwhelmed and just needed a minute to breathe. *Life was messy.* But for those few hours, none of that mattered. It was just me and my son. Soaking up those first minutes of his life. Holding him. Letting it sink in. Every one of my kids has brought me to tears when they were born, those moments are timeless and powerful. Hard to describe.

Britney was nothing but supportive. That was one thing about her: she was always 100 percent behind me as a father. She'd seen how I was with Kori, and she knew the kind of dad I was going to be. That meant something to her. But what hit me hard was the reality: I wasn't going to be able to see Kaleb every day. He was just a baby, and Shar wasn't about to hand him over for long stretches anytime soon. That was tough. I love being around my kids. And not having that, especially at the start, was one of the hardest parts of those early months. When Kori was a newborn, I was there every day. I got to experience all those little changes: the sounds, the laughs, the way they sleep on your chest. Those moments go by fast. And I didn't want to miss them all with Kaleb.

But I was determined to make it work. My parents were living in Oceanside then, and I knew they'd help any way they could. I just had to focus on being the best dad I could be, even if the circumstances weren't ideal.

And through all of that, Britney and I were still moving forward with the wedding. Life didn't slow down. It kept coming, wave after wave.

We got married in September. Five months after we got engaged. Five months. (More on this later.) Way shorter than the five years I used to think I'd need to figure marriage out. But it fit. That was our lifestyle back then. Everything was moving a million miles an hour.

CHAPTER SEVEN

There were a couple of times early on where I could tell Britney still had some unfinished business with Justin Timberlake. It didn't come up often, but it lingered, like a ghost in the background of our relationship.

And I'll never forget the night before we got married.

We were staying in one of the bungalows at the Fairmont in Santa Monica. It was supposed to be our moment of calm before the storm. Just us, getting ready to take this next step in our lives. I remember jumping in the shower, and when I got out, she wasn't in the room. I looked around, checked the balcony, nothing. Tried calling her. No answer. That's when I walked out to the front of the bungalow.

And there she was, sitting out by the planters, leaning up against one of the brick walls that faced the street. It's all enclosed, so it wasn't like she was out in public, but still, it felt off. She was on the phone. I figured she was talking to her mom or her sister, so I went back to the room.

When she got back to the room, I could tell she'd been crying. I asked her, "Are you okay? What was that about?" She said she was talking to Justin. She said she needed to call him, to end one chapter of her life before starting a new one. You can imagine my shock, the night before we were supposed to get married. I told her straight up, "If you're not ready to do this, we don't have to. We don't need to get married. I'm happy with what we have."

I meant it. Marriage wasn't some big thing for me. I was young. She told me she was ready to get married and wanted the wedding to happen fast. I would've been fine figuring things out with her before taking that step. But she insisted it wasn't about second thoughts or doubts. She just wanted closure with him, to end things on good terms. She said they hadn't talked much since everything went down between them. And I believed her. At least, I wanted to.

Even after the wedding, I could tell she hadn't fully moved on. It wasn't like she was constantly bringing him up, but it came up enough. I could see that part of her heart still had ties to him. At the time, I chalked it up to her needing closure. I wasn't mad. I understood. That's what happens when someone was a big part of your life for so long.

But now, looking back, especially after hearing what she said in her book, I realize it was deeper than that. She never really got over him. She might've loved me, but there was always something there with Justin that she couldn't let go of.

Being in love with someone still hanging on to someone else—you feel it, even if they don't say it. It's not something you can compete with. It's just there, like this invisible wall between you. And that night before our wedding, when she was on the phone with him, I think I knew. I just didn't want to admit it to myself.

The wedding was supposed to be this grand affair. Originally, we planned a big celebration, 250 guests, maybe more. All our families, all our friends. Britney's dream wedding.

Then the press found out.

They somehow got all of the details: that it was at Bacara, the date, everything. Someone had leaked it to them. Our privacy, our special day, was gone. She and I sat down, frustrated and anxious, trying to figure out what to do next. She didn't want to go through with it at the original venue anymore, and honestly, I couldn't blame her. The dream wedding was off.

We decided to pivot.

Her wedding planner turned out to be solid under pressure. She came up with the idea to downsize, keep it intimate and secretive. No leaks. No frenzy. Just the people who mattered most. That's how we landed on a small, private wedding in September, much earlier than we'd originally planned. The location was a gorgeous house tucked away in Studio City. No one outside our closest circle knew about it. In fact, none of the guests even realized they were attending a wedding until the night before.

Here's how we pulled it off:

Everyone who was invited thought they were in town for wedding preparations—dress and suit fittings, a rehearsal. On Saturday, I took the guys out for a round of golf, and she took the girls out for a spa day. When we all reunited that evening, we dropped the bombshell:

"We're getting married tomorrow!"

There was a pause, then confusion, then excitement lit up their faces. We told them the fittings had all been part of the plan. Their outfits would be in their rooms by morning, and shuttles would take them to the venue.

Sunday arrived, and everything fell into place.

The guest list was tight, maybe forty or fifty people. Just immediate family and closest friends. Her family flew in from Louisiana; my brothers and lifelong friends were there. It was intimate, it was special, and it was ours.

Of course, the paparazzi eventually caught on. They trailed us to the house, circling like vultures. But by then, it didn't matter. We had created a moment that felt untouched by the spectacle outside. It might not have been the wedding we originally envisioned, but in many ways, it was better. It was just us, surrounded by the people we loved most.

When we took off on our honeymoon to Fiji, I thought I knew what to expect. I'd been around the world and seen some wild places, but this was on another level. We stayed at this place called Turtle Island. This wasn't your typical five-star luxury resort. It was like stepping into another world. No TVs, no phones, just one landline in the main hut. There were about twenty villas, all beachfront, and the whole island was pure simplicity. They grew their own food, fished for the day's meals, and traded with nearby islands for anything else they needed. No livestock, no grocery stores, just fresh, clean living.

At first, it was a shock to the system. Coming from the fast-paced, insane grind of life back in Los Angeles, we were like fish out of water. I mean, by the third day, we were ready to bounce. No movies, no takeout, no distractions—just us, the beach, and a lot of quiet. But we stuck it out, and something incredible happened. Once we got over that initial restlessness, we really started to *be* there. We went fishing, swam in the clearest water you've ever seen, explored the island, and even started hanging out with the other couples.

By the end of the ten days, we didn't want to go. We were bawling our eyes out. Being so cut off from everything else forced us to genuinely connect—to talk, to share, to just *be* together. I think it was one of the most important experiences we had as a couple. We came back stronger, closer, and ready for the next chapter.

Returning to reality, we landed right back in the fast lane. We were shuttling back and forth between Los Angeles and Britney's hometown of Kentwood, Louisiana, as well as searching for our new house.

A few months later, we found out Britney was pregnant with Preston. Discovering we were going to be parents was unforgettable, a head-over-heels kind of happiness.

She was glowing, radiant with joy. That time was all about us, building our relationship, dreaming about the future, and getting ready for our little boy. Everything felt new and exciting, and we were in this perfect bubble of love and anticipation. I'm proud of that chapter in my life. I was there for Britney whenever she needed me. I already loved being a father and felt blessed to have a third baby on the way. It was a time when everything felt possible, and we were just two people in love, figuring it all out together.

CHAPTER EIGHT

alibu felt like our "golden years," and the house we bought there was a big part of that. For the first time in our relationship, we had something that was truly ours. Before we got married, we signed our deal for the TV show *Chaotic*, a reality series about Britney's life on the road and our relationship. That deal gave me the money to help buy the house. The show aired while Britney was pregnant with Preston. We both put money down and bought it together. Up until then, we'd only lived in places she owned before we got together. It meant a lot to me, being able to contribute financially to a home we shared.

It took a while to find the right house, but as soon as we saw this one, we knew—it was home. It already had kids' rooms, one of them totally set up for a toddler. We knew that would be Preston's room. He was coming soon. Right away, we started planning renovations. Britney wanted to focus on the inside, remodeling the kitchen, hiring interior designers, while I took on the backyard. Yes, me, I was mowing the fucking lawn. No shit, the backyard became my masterpiece.

We tore that place apart and rebuilt it from the ground up. I became, like, the unofficial general contractor. I put in a pool with a swim-up bar and a grotto, a waterfall with a slide and a rock to jump off, and a barbecue area with TVs and a firepit. The perfect setup for hanging out or entertaining. I wanted a space where we could really live, where family and friends could come together and have a good time. That was my dream project. I put everything into it. I was laying stone and planting grass, but more than that I was laying the groundwork for the next twenty years of our lives. I pictured family barbecues, kids running around, music playing, drinks flowing. For the first time in a long time, it felt like we were planting roots, not just moving in somewhere. We were creating something. A real home.

Then came Preston. Our first child together.

Everything about his birth was different than what I'd experienced before.

When Kori and Kaleb were born, it was this big family moment. Everyone was there. My parents, Shar's family, and the room was full of love and support. That's how I thought it always went. But with Preston, it wasn't like that.

We had to plan everything down to the minute. Paparazzi were posted outside our house daily. Helicopters overhead. A simple

Starbucks run turned into a media circus. We knew we couldn't risk any surprise hospital visits, so we scheduled a C-section for September 14.

The day came and it was just me, Britney, and a couple of our security guys outside the room. Inside, it was just the two of us.

Once they pulled that curtain up and started the procedure, everything else faded. I remember catching glimpses of what was happening behind the sheet, just flashes, and then hearing Preston's cry for the first time. Man…he came out looking like the definition of a perfect baby. No cone head, no bruising, just smooth, peaceful, and already camera-ready.

But what really hit me wasn't even Preston. It was Britney's face. I'd never seen her like that before. Ever. Pure joy, undeniable love, tears pouring down her face. It is one of those memories burned into my mind, something I still hold onto through all the turmoil that followed.

So yeah, we were riding this high. Life felt full. Preston had just been born, and everything was still new and exciting, and then—*bam*—we found out Britney was pregnant again. I think it was only a few months after Preston was born. Total shock. But honestly? We were both thrilled.

We just looked at each other, like, "Well, damn, if we play this right, we could be done after this one." Two kids, back to back. Britney was really hoping for a girl that time, too, thought we might get the pair, boy and girl. Obviously, it didn't turn out that way, but it didn't matter. We were simply excited to grow the family.

I always let the mother pick the baby names. I would give my input, but she chose the names, and I was cool with it. With her, it was also this real southern tradition; the first and middle names were everything. That's how the whole family referred to people. Preston was always "Sean Preston" or "Sean P.," and Jayden was "Jayden James"—"JJ" for short. Same thing with her and her family: Britney Jean, Jamie Lynn. That was how they rolled.

Jayden's birth came a lot like Preston's. Same plan, different hospital. Preston had been born in Santa Monica, but for Jayden, we went to Cedars-Sinai. Same doctors, same setup, scheduled C-section, fully orchestrated, because there was no way we could do anything low-key at that point. It was still pandemonium outside. Paparazzi, helicopters, people following us to Starbucks. So we planned it all again.

Funny how certain details stick with you. I remember the doctor straight up saying, "We're not doing September 11. No way." And we were like, "Yeah, no question." So Jayden came September 12, two days before Preston's first birthday. Crazy how tight that window was. Irish twins, basically.

The birth itself was calm. Same as with Preston, just me and her in the room. Britney didn't want anyone else. Jayden was perfect. Like all my kids. And yeah, things were already starting to get bumpy behind the scenes. (Stuff we'll get into later.) But I didn't want to bury his story under all that. Because Jayden, like all my kids, was born from love. Every single one of them. And that's what I hold onto when I think back. Through everything, they were born out of love.

Once we were settled into our Malibu home, everything felt like it was moving upward. That stretch of time was steady. Positive. We didn't have many lows.

CHAPTER NINE

All might have been quiet on the home front, but the barbarians were still at the gates. A whole army of paparazzi, lying in wait for two years straight. Like our very own private press corps. It wasn't only at events or special occasions. It was every single day. Whether we were running errands, going out to eat, or simply trying to live our lives, there they were. Sometimes, it felt like we had a horde of street kids following us around, except these "kids" were grown adults with cameras and an unhealthy obsession with our every move, documenting every moment. It was exhausting, but I learned to navigate it. Some of those guys were only doing their jobs, and I didn't blame them for that. But there were others who pushed every limit, and they're the ones who made life feel like a circus. Through it all, I kept my patience. Most of the time. It wasn't easy, but I knew that losing my cool would only give them what they wanted. And that wasn't a price I was willing to pay.

Just the sheer scale of it all was a huge eye-opener. Before experiencing it firsthand, I had no idea just how invasive and hectic it could get. Paparazzi weren't just a few guys snapping pictures. They were a mob. On any given day, there could be twenty, thirty, or even fifty of them swarming us. The night of our wedding was one of the worst. After the ceremony, we decided to head out to a club to celebrate. On the way, we stopped at a red light, and in a blink, paparazzi jumped out of their cars, blocking oncoming traffic, trying to get pictures of us inside the vehicle. It was so bad that my security guard, Lonnie, lost it.

I had never seen him that enraged before. He jumped out of the car and turned into a fucking raging bull. He didn't hurt anyone, but his sheer fury made every single one of those guys retreat back to their cars. In that moment, I realized the line between safety and anarchy could get blurry fast. They were putting people in danger just to get a shot of us sitting in a goddamn car.

It wasn't just L.A. or New York, either. It was even worse overseas. In Europe, the paparazzi seemed to multiply. Every outing was a gamble. Sometimes, we'd manage to sneak away for a couple of hours, but they always found us eventually. They caused wrecks, people got hurt, and the mob-like atmosphere around us never seemed to let up.

One of my most insane paparazzi run-ins didn't even involve Britney. It happened in Vegas. I had gone there for a friend's birthday, setting up a night at Crazy Horse, a strip club, for about thirty of us. I wasn't in the mood to party; I just wanted to set my friends up, make sure they had a great time, and leave. I told everyone I'd only stay for twenty minutes. My plan was to say my hellos, have a drink, tip the staff, and head back to the hotel to play craps.

As I was leaving with my security guard, Big Mike, trailing just a little bit behind me, a stripper came out of nowhere and put her arm around my neck. I turned to look at her, caught off guard, and my gaze just so happened to land on her chest— right as a paparazzo snapped a picture. This wasn't some rando paparazzo. This fucker had set the whole thing up. He'd been waiting, camera-ready, for that exact moment, probably paid the girl, so he could ambush me and get something worth getting, even if it was bullshit. That picture would've been gold—me, mid-turn, staring at this woman's breasts. That kind of shot could easily have sold for a quarter of a million dollars, maybe more.

Big Mike saw what was happening, and all hell broke loose. He and my friends took off after the paparazzo, who bolted out of the club. My boys weren't playing around, a bunch of them chased this guy around the block. In a panic, he threw his camera into a bush and ran back to the club, screaming to the security guards that he was afraid for his life.

Meanwhile, Big Mike threw me in a cab, shouting at the driver to get me the hell out of there. But me, being the dumbass I was, told the driver to circle back. I wanted to see what was happening. Big Mike spotted me in the cab, and he was pissed. He yelled at me to get the fuck out of there. I finally listened, and headed back to the hotel.

When my friends got back, they had the paparazzo's camera. We looked through the photos on the memory card before destroying it, and sure enough, there it was: a perfect shot of me turning my head, caught in the act of looking at the girl's chest. It was all so staged and sleazy. That guy was willing to break the law, and maybe his jaw, just to set me up and sell that image. The whole experience was a reminder of just how relentless paparazzi could be back then. Not only did they want the shot; they wanted to create a narrative, manufacture moments, and exploit them for profit. And for me, it was a massive wake-up call. Even when I was simply trying to help my friends celebrate, the paparazzi found a way to make it into a scandal. Make me a villain. So maybe I leaned into it, because in a way, it was like having this alternate persona I could step into when needed while keeping my real self private. Sure, the paparazzi tried to invade that privacy, grabbing pieces and snapshots of my life, but the truth is, they never really knew me. Nobody outside my circle does. That separation helped me deal with everything that came with the spotlight.

Over time, you get numb to it. The flashbulbs, the shouts, it all becomes part of your daily life. You know that when you step out, there's going to be a swarm of photographers tailing you wherever you go. Even when I wasn't with her, they were still there. It got to the point where sometimes I'd think, *Nah, I don't feel like going out today. Not worth it.*

So you end up secluding yourself.

Thank God for that house in Malibu. It was massive, a beautiful crib with a pool and everything I needed to keep myself occupied. When the outside world felt too overwhelming, at least we had that sanctuary. I could stay home without feeling like I was losing my mind, without feeling trapped. It became our escape from the madness outside.

We lived in a gated community, and while that did offer some privacy, it still wasn't enough to keep the paparazzi fully at bay. It wasn't uncommon to see dozens of photographers stationed outside the gates, waiting for someone, anyone, to make a move. We weren't the only ones under siege. Our neighbors included a lot of big names who drew just as much attention—Mel Gibson, Matthew Perry, and many others.

The sheriff's department in Malibu was a blessing. They had been dealing with the paparazzi circus for years because of all the high-profile residents, and they knew how to handle it. They were incredibly understanding of the situation, stepping in when things got out of hand. If I was driving and the paparazzi were swarming, the deputies didn't hesitate to pull up and ask if I needed help. One time, I was driving my Ferrari on PCH, and a motorcycle cop pulled up beside me at the light. He looked back at the paparazzi trailing me and asked, "You need some help?" When I nodded, he flashed a grin and said, "How fast does that thing go?"

The light turned green, and we gunned it.

For a moment, it felt like freedom, just me and the cop tearing up the road while the paparazzi sat frozen at the light. But when his bike started to wobble at high speed, I let off the gas. Not worth the risk.

Sometimes, a simple look from cops was all it took to make the photographers back off. Other times, the paps didn't even care if the cops were there. We'd show our gratitude in small ways, donating money to help them upgrade their gym equipment or office gear. It wasn't a bribe or anything like that, just a donation to the fund.

We were extremely grateful for the job they did, especially since our security team had to coordinate with them regularly, because if it wasn't the paparazzi they were heading off at the pass, it was some unhinged stalker.

I'll never forget the morning a man from Germany showed up at our front gate, screaming that Britney was his wife, and those were his kids. The look in his eyes was chilling—pure madness. He sat on top of a pillar at the gate, shouting and ranting, and I remember thinking: *If he jumps down, I need to run because this guy will slit my throat.*

Our security team had a huge mugshot book of people they had to watch out for—stalkers, obsessive fans, threats. Before I met Britney, I never really thought about how intense that side of fame could be. But when you're living it, you realize how real and dangerous it is. It made me understand why security was absolutely necessary. It also made me very thankful to the guys on our protection detail. They were like family to me. I'd known most of them for years. Even before Britney and I were together.

The frenzy went next-level when our kids were born. At the time, a photo of Preston or Jayden was worth over a million dollars. That kind of money turns photographers into predators, willing to do anything to get the shot. I mean, think about it: that one shot could set a pap up for life. It was much more than simply annoying; it was life-threatening. We eventually decided to release the first photos of the boys ourselves to kill the frenzy. It wasn't an easy decision. Neither of us wanted to give up that moment, but the alternative was far worse. We talked it over with security, and it became clear that releasing the photos was the safest option. It might not back the paparazzi off completely, but it would take away the dangerous desperation that led to the kind of car chases that could get people killed. I mean, these guys were as reckless as they were lawless. They'd break every traffic rule in the book to get the shot, running red lights, blocking other vehicles, weaving through lanes. It didn't matter if they endangered themselves or others. I remember one time in Venice when a paparazzo got hit by a car, because he wasn't paying attention while chasing a celebrity. It wasn't an isolated incident. The same thing happened with Bieber's crew. It was pure madness, and it happened all the time.

The worst part was that it wasn't only big events or nights out that drew them. Going to the grocery store, grabbing lunch at Moonshadows, sitting on our patio, they were there, cameras in hand, ready to turn the mundane into a spectacle. Other than exclusive wedding and baby-type photos, I still don't understand how they made money when there were forty of them snapping the same shot of us walking out of Subway a thousand times over. How could they call it exclusive when the same image was flooding every tabloid? But I guess that's the frenzy. They'd fight tooth and nail for even the slightest edge, making it all up as they went along.

CHAPTER TEN

Fame didn't change me in the ways people might assume. Sure, it gave me confidence; and to some, maybe that confidence came across as cockiness. Confidence over cockiness has always been my mantra. But man, seeing some of that stuff now, I can understand how it came off. I look back to those days, when maybe the spotlight was a little too bright, blinding me. And now that I can see more clearly, I can't help but cringe a little. I don't think I was trying to be someone I wasn't. I was being me, but I was also leaning heavily into this artist persona I was trying to build. I was playing a role in some ways, trying to figure out who I was in the public eye, which sometimes meant putting on a show, even if it wasn't the realest version of me.

To a lot of people, I probably looked like an arrogant asshole. And that's not an easy pill to swallow. Now, in my mid-forties,

I can look back at that younger version of myself and see why people might have thought I was full of it. I get it. To some, I probably came off like I thought I was God's gift to the world. But the truth is, I was just trying to figure it all out as I went, making mistakes, learning, growing, like anyone else. Except, I was doing it all under a microscope.

The thing is, a lot of what I was going through back then wasn't visible to anyone but me. The nervousness I felt in interviews, the anxiety that would creep in before stepping on stage, it wasn't new. I'd dealt with that for years, even dating back to my dancing days. But back then, I didn't know how to handle it. I didn't have the tools or the perspective to navigate those moments with grace. Now, with years of life experience under my belt, I can sit in an interview, stay calm, think through my words, and approach things differently. But back then? I was just winging it.

Once, I did this Virgin Mobile charity gig with Richard Branson in Times Square, stepping out of an armored truck in Abraham Lincoln masks to face a crowd of 5000. Nervously grabbing the mic, I shouted, "We're doing it big in '96!"—oblivious that it was 2006, not 1996—while my security guy, Big Mike, shot me a bewildered look. So yeah, you could say I was pretty green at public speaking.

Fame itself wasn't what drove my decisions or changed who I was at my core. It was never the objective, never the endgame. What fame did do was magnify everything, every win and every mistake. If I'd been chasing fame, staying with Britney would've been the obvious move. Pushing away from that would've been unthinkable for someone addicted to the attention. But the truth is, I had already hit a wall. She may have been the one who technically walked out, but I was already gone. I'm not saying it wasn't exhilarating, being thrust into the limelight at twenty-five. It was the ultimate rush, an adrenaline high like nothing else. It felt like I was on top of the world, ready to conquer anything. Fame, in a way, was the most powerful drug I'd ever experienced. It was intoxicating, addictive, and dangerous. You feel invincible. But the truth is, fame is a double-edged sword. It can empower you, but it can also consume you. This was a different time, before social media took over, but I was still everywhere. For two straight years, I was in nearly every tabloid magazine, every single week. There was no escaping it. The spotlight was relentless; and eventually, it took a toll.

I wasn't just famous—I was infamous. The minute Shar spoke out, revealing that I had left her for Britney while she was pregnant, I became "America's Bad Boy." The tabloids feasted on the narrative, and the public was quick to form their own opinions. Suddenly, my every move was subject to worldwide scrutiny, and the headlines weren't exactly kind. I remember my dad, Mike, being pissed off all the time, always saying he wanted to give the press a piece of his mind. I couldn't blame him. He knows who I really am, and watching me get painted as something I wasn't was hard for him. Hell, it was hard for everyone who knew me, friends, family, all of them. I kept having to tell him it wasn't worth it, that it would only make things worse. Maybe that's the passive side of me, just letting things roll off, trying not to make a bad situation worse.

I learned the hard way that there's a distinct difference between being famous and being infamous. For me, infamy meant walking into rooms where people already had a preconceived notion of who I was. They'd read the headlines, seen the stories, and made up their minds before ever meeting me. But here's the thing: when I did get the chance to sit down with someone, to talk to them face-to-face, the narrative changed. Time and time again, people would say, "You're nothing like what I thought you'd be."

That contrast followed me everywhere. In some ways, it worked to my advantage. Booking gigs as the bad guy, or in meetings when suits and producers would be skeptical, but once they spent time with me, they saw who I really was. Still, there was always this uphill battle to overcome the assumptions, to prove I wasn't the tabloid villain people expected. This made it really difficult to build my own brand.

The gossip, the rumors, and the public ridicule, it's all like a high school drama on a massive scale. And while I was lucky to have a strong sense of self by the time fame hit, there were still moments that got to me. What hurt the most wasn't the odd fan or even Britney's most loyal supporters. I expected them to be upset, to lash out. What stung was when people in the industry, the so-called Hollywood elites, jumped on the bandwagon

77

without knowing me at all. When someone like Ben Stiller or Rosie O'Donnell makes a jab, it feels personal. It'd be one thing if they were strangers, but these were people in the same world, people who should understand how damaging words can be. They had no clue who I really was, yet still felt entitled to publicly judge me. I was an easy target. I came into this world suddenly, attached to one of the biggest stars on the planet, and to everyone else, I was just some random guy riding her coattails. They didn't know me. They didn't care to know me. But that didn't stop them from piling on. I mean, yeah, it's easy to laugh it off now, but back then, hearing Jimmy Kimmel or whoever else make a joke at my expense did bother me. It wasn't devastating, but it was frustrating. It made me feel like I was stuck in this caricature, like my life was some kind of Jerry Springer episode for people to laugh at. Jimmy Kimmel's bit, where he literally put me in a box and threw it into the ocean? That's exactly how it felt. That moment summed up how the industry treated me, like I was something to be laughed at, thrown away, and forgotten. That hurt. It's one thing to deal with the tabloids, but it's another when the ridicule comes from people you once respected or people who should know better.

CHAPTER ELEVEN

G rowing up, I'd dealt with my fair share of challenges. I wasn't a stranger to people talking behind my back or making assumptions. In middle school, my yearbook superlative was: *Most Likely to Be on America's Most Wanted.*

When I was ten, I started acting out, sneaking around with older girls, getting into trouble. My mom decided it'd be better for me to live with my dad back in Fresno, and I agreed. At the time, I blamed her for the divorce, mostly because I didn't know any better. My dad had remarried Colette, who had two kids from a previous marriage: my brother Dustin, about four years older than me, and my sister Nikki, who was the same age as I was. Around thirteen, my life started shifting the way it does for a lot of teenagers. That's when I hit middle school. I'd been held back in first grade, so I was older than all of the kids in my class. Dustin was already in high school, and to me, he was larger than life, the epitome of cool. I used to sneak into his room and steal his clothes when he wasn't around. Before long, I was shadowing him, copying everything he did. I was only thirteen, but I thought I was already grown.

I was also experimenting with things I probably shouldn't have been. That's when I smoked weed for the first time. I remember going to one of my brother's friends and buying three joints. He told me, "The first one probably won't work, maybe not even the second. It takes a few times to actually get high." I was already smoking cigarettes and doing stupid stuff. But when I finally got high for the first time, that was it—my first love, Mary J. Drinking, on the other hand, didn't sit right. One time, a friend's mom was out of town, and we got into her stash of Cuervo 1800. I got hammered and ended up puking my guts out, so I swore off alcohol for a while. Weed was different. It only lasted an hour, and never made me sick or feel out of control. Back in those days, it was mostly seedy brick weed and on occasion you'd come across "the Chronic" or "primo," as we called it.

I liked hanging out with the older kids. My brother had this friend, Graham, who drove a Cutlass. One day, I ditched school to tag along. We were cruising through the neighborhood when Graham pulled out a three-foot bong. I'd never hit one before, so I didn't know what I was doing, or what to expect. I took a giant rip, and the smoke hit my lungs like tear gas. I coughed and sneezed at the same time, blowing the cherry straight out of the bowl. It landed on Graham's neck while he was driving, and he swerved across the road, tires screeching. I was gasping for air, snot hanging from my nose, ash all over my lap, and everyone in the car was staring at me like I'd just exploded. Then the snot sucked back up my face in one clean snap, and we all lost it. Just died laughing. One of those classic high moments, too ridiculous not to be hilarious.

At least it was hilarious until we pulled into Graham's place, still hotboxing the car, and my dad's truck came screeching up beside us. He jumped out, stormed over, yanked the door open, and ripped me out by the shirt, tossing me into his cab. Graham and my brother got off scot-free, leaving me to wonder why I always seemed to draw the short straw.

By the time I was sixteen, I'd already moved on from just smoking weed to trying other things. Mushrooms became a favorite for a while, until I had a bad trip. I tried coke, acid and speed. It was all part of being a teenager and experimenting. I also got into selling weed, though I wasn't great at it. I smoked too much of my own supply, and my profits barely covered what I owed.

It was around then that I met Talon. He was nineteen, a little person who had just gotten out of jail for selling acid at school when he was seventeen. He may have been small, but he walked around like he was six-five. He was charged as an adult and ended up doing seven months in Wasco. Talon was a good dude, though he'd had a rough life. He was on disability, trying to make ends meet, and we became tight. Talon's apartment turned into the trap house. People were in and out constantly, buying whatever they needed. I'd go there to hang out and grab what I needed, but over time, I started to realize how hot his place was getting. Not good if you're trying to be discreet.

One night, about five or six of us were all hanging out at Talon's place, just chilling, passing time, as the usual steady stream of people came by to pick up. Talon had a sliding glass door near the front of his apartment, and it was always cracked open because the place would get hot from being so busy and packed with people. Someone was always coming in or out.

But then suddenly, two guys jumped through that sliding door. They had masks on, one was holding a shotgun, the other a small handgun, maybe a .380. They yelled at us to get on the ground. I froze for a second before hitting the floor, heart drumming through my chest. They were shouting and cursing, making it clear they weren't playing around. They grabbed Talon, put him on the ground, threw a pillow over his head, and told him to give up his shit.

Then one guy held us at gunpoint, while the other ransacked the apartment. They took everyone's cash, made us empty our pockets, and then dragged Talon to the backroom where he kept his safe. Talon tried to downplay his bank, but they tore through everything, taking every last dollar and gram they could find. I could hear Talon pleading with them, but they just ignored him.

It lasted maybe ten minutes, but it stretched like hours. When they bolted, the silence crashed over us like a nuclear blastwave.

As soon as they left and the shock wore off, the anger set in. Talon was on the phone with some of his people getting the crew together to find out who did this. I was still finishing watching my life flash before my eyes. Some of the others ran out to see if they could catch up to them. Talon looked at me and told me to get the hell outta there. I was seventeen at the time, and he knew I wasn't trying to stick around to see what came next. I mean, I've seen a lot of shit up to this point but never had a gun in my face.

After that, I kept my distance. I'd see Talon and the crew occasionally, but I avoided the apartment for a few months. Then, one night, I stopped by to pick up some stuff. The place was packed, about thirty people crammed into a tiny space. Talon had recently come into possession of some stolen nitrous tanks from a local dentist, and the crew were partying hard, hitting nitrous and getting high.

Around nine p.m., there was a knock at the door. Everyone assumed it was another buyer, but when someone cracked the door open, two guys pushed their way into the place. This time, one of them had no mask—not a good sign. They kicked the door open and immediately started shouting at us, waving their guns around, just like last time. They herded everyone into the backroom, cramming us together like cattle. One guy watched the door while the other took Talon aside, held a gun to his head, and forced him to answer the door for any new arrivals. They'd drag in anyone who showed up, rob them, and throw them into the backroom with us. It went on like that for almost an hour. I remember one guy in the room with us, Farnham, was ready to fight back. He was amped, shifting his weight, reaching to pull a gun from his waistband while still lying on the floor. You could see it in his eyes. He was gearing up to do something reckless. I just looked at him and shook my head. This wasn't the time to play superhero. I had to whisper, "Don't. You'll get us all killed."

Eventually, they left. My boy D grabbed a shotgun from under the couch cushions and told me to pull around back. Fueled by adrenaline and rage, I didn't even hesitate. I ran out, jumped in my '87 Honda CRX, and picked him up from the alley. He said he recognized one of the guys who jacked us and told me to head toward a neighborhood a few blocks away.

As we got closer, my mind running a million miles an hour, I realized that this wasn't the kind of situation I wanted to be in. I told D, "I don't think I can do this shit." He said, "Don't worry. If it gets real, just drop me off at their spot." This dude was a real one.

Luckily, that's not how it went down.

We pulled up to their apartment. He jumped out, ran around back, and came back less than a minute later. Nobody was there. I was instantly relieved. I dropped him back at Talon's spot and bounced.

On my way home, the adrenaline started wearing off, and that's when the consequences hit me. My whole life could've been derailed over something I wasn't even directly involved in.

That was the moment I knew I couldn't go back. I called Talon a few days later and told him, "You need to get out of there. You've got a target on your back." He didn't listen. A few months later, he got arrested—for drugs, and for the stolen nitrous tanks they threw away in the dumpster out back. The DEA had been watching him the whole time, just waiting for an excuse. They probably saw the whole robbery take place. Maybe he was lucky it was the cops instead of more criminals. Fresno was wild back then.

After that, I cut ties with everyone. I moved out of my apartment and back in with my parents for a while to reset. I realized real quick that I wasn't about that life. The trauma of those robberies stayed with me. I began suffering panic attacks, especially when I smoked. At the time, I thought it was just the weed or the cigarettes, but now I realize it was the lingering anxiety from having guns pointed at my head—twice. That's not the kind of thing you just walk away from clean. Every time I took a hit, I felt like my chest was caving in, and I couldn't figure out why.

When I finally moved out again, I decided to do something that felt safer and more under my control. I got a two-bedroom apartment and started growing weed. And here's the kicker: my *mom*, who lived up in Oregon, became my supplier. Now, most moms would send you care packages with cookies or a little extra cash. Not my mom. She was like, "Oh, you're gonna grow? Cool. Come up here and get some clones." I drove up there, and she walked me down to her basement like she was showing me family heirlooms. "Here's the good stuff, Skunk Number One and Northern Lights hybrid," she said, pointing to rows of plants like a proud parent at a science fair.

I couldn't believe it. My mom wasn't just supportive, she was like the unofficial CEO of my tiny operation. She even gave me the whole playbook on how to care for the plants. I duct-taped a fluorescent light to the inside of my trunk to keep the clones alive for the drive back to California. Picture this: me, driving south on I-5, a glowing trunk full of weed plants. If I'd been pulled over, I don't even know how I would have explained it. "Officer, I swear, my mom made me do it…"

Once I got back to Fresno, I set up shop. It wasn't a huge operation, just a single room with enough plants to grow a couple of pounds every six to eight weeks. I absolutely loved growing. I did it for a couple of years, and only my family and my girlfriend at the time knew where I lived. I kept everything tight, super low-key. I was careful not to end up in the same kind of situation Talon had. I'd keep half for myself and sell the rest to just one person. That way, I could fly under the radar and avoid any unwanted attention. I wasn't exactly balling, but a few extra thousand here and there made a big difference. It paid for trips, nights out, and meant I never had to worry about buying weed. My day job at the pizza place covered rent and bills, so this was just a side hustle, but a damn good one.

About a year after Jimmy and I reconnected, I finally brought him over. It was a couple of days before harvest, and until then, he had no idea where I lived, let alone that I had a whole room full of fire. He'd been asking stuff like, "Yo, how come you never let me chill at your place?" So when I finally did, he walks in and goes, "So this is where you live? Dope spot."

I walked him to the grow room and opened the door.

He dropped to his knees like he'd just seen a religious vision, lay down, and started humping the floor. I guess you could say he was a little excited. It was like watching a kid at Christmas get that first glimpse of the gifts under the tree—except in this case, the gift was the trees.

It was hilarious. And honestly, I could completely relate.

But it wasn't long before my life veered down a different path.

I'd reconnected with my best friend, Jimmy, threw myself back into my dancing, and wound up marrying one of the biggest pop stars on the planet, as our relationship played out on the front pages of the world's tabloid press. What kept me grounded was my sense of self and my values. All that past behind me, dealing with rumors and assumptions early on, slanging weed, getting robbed at gunpoint, that kind of experience toughens you up. Fame is a beast, both alluring and destructive, but it didn't change who I was at my core. I've held onto who I am. I've made mistakes, and I've faced the consequences, but I've also grown. And that's what I hope people take away from all of this, not just the headlines or the drama, but the journey of a man navigating life under an unforgiving spotlight. I've always tried to be a good person, to show respect, and to take care of the people around me. That's something I take pride in, even when the world is quick to tear you down.

CHAPTER TWELVE

B eing with someone who has bottomless pockets is… complicated. Growing up in the late seventies and eighties, I had this old-school idea of what a "breadwinner" was. Both of my parents worked; but in my mind, I saw my grandpa going to work while my grandma stayed home with the grandkids. That image stuck with me, even as the world changed. I was with someone who could provide for generations of our family, but I still wanted to bring something to the table. Even though I knew I would never be in the same tax bracket.

She was supportive—or at least acted supportive—of me wanting to do music, act, and explore the entertainment industry. That had always been my goal. I left Fresno for L.A. to be part of the industry, to experience it all. Even back then, while I was dancing, I was always freestyling, messing around with music in my car. Music and dance—they go hand in hand. Dancing gave me rhythm and timing, a connection to sound that felt instinctive. It was in me from birth. When I was in L.A. before Britney, I had worked with a few producers, been in recording studios, and had this itch to see what I could create.

Fast forward to selling our show *Chaotic*. With some money in the bank, I could finally afford studio time and producers. Britney was pregnant, but she supported me diving into music. That's when I started working with Disco D. This dude was wild, a bipolar genius who worked with 50 Cent. Later, I worked with JR, who had collaborated with Britney. I know now that I should've taken my time, put in those 10,000 hours and really honed my craft. But back then, I wasn't thinking like that. I had this blind optimism, like, *yeah, this is good enough—let's go!* I wasn't seeing the big picture yet. All I wanted to do was create and share—to put my art out into the world and have people hear it—without thinking about whether it was truly ready.

I spent a lot of time going back and forth to studios in Santa Monica. I loved it. But I hated being away from my family. That's when I told Britney I wanted to build a studio in the house. She was all for it.

I went all out: an SSL 900 mixing board, a vocal booth, racks of equipment. It was a legit setup, and it meant I could work from home. Preston was just a baby, and I wanted to be there for him. Plus, it made things easier for Britney if she wanted to record, it was all right there.

Working from home, I started collaborating with new people. C-Note was an up and coming producer who had an incredible sound. Also this kid from the Bay called Ya Boy. YB was crazy talented, and we did most of that first album together. During that time, I jumped on one of Game's mixtapes, not even a full verse. Not long after, I got a call from 50 Cent asking if I'd be down to hop on his mixtape. I ended up turning him down because I was rolling with The Game and some of the Black Wall Street guys. I thought I was being loyal. But the truth is, their beef had nothing to do with me, and I wasn't wise enough in the ways of the business to see that yet.

50 probably thought I was a dumbass, and I kind of was. I should've jumped on the first flight to New York. Looking back, I realize how much more valuable it would've been to have someone in my corner who really understood the ins and outs of the hip-hop world. Instead, I tried to do the whole thing on my own.

But honestly, I didn't expect my work to get destroyed the way it did. Sure, I knew people might roll their eyes and go: *Oh, Britney's husband thinks he's a musician now. Cute.* I was prepared for some of that. But what I wasn't ready for was how fucking brutal it was. This wasn't just a little shade; it was a full-on eclipse. People killed it. I didn't think I'd be the next big thing, but I also didn't expect the world to be waiting in ambush with their knives sharpened. And look, I know what people were saying: *He's just riding her coattails...*or: *He wouldn't have a career if he wasn't married to* *her.* Trust me, I heard it all. And maybe there was some truth to that. But for me, it was never about trying to prove something to anyone else. I just wanted to do something I loved.

That first album was a wake-up call. It wasn't just some project I worked hard on; it was something I believed in. I poured my heart into it, and when it didn't perform the way I'd hoped, it hurt. It was humbling though. I thought people would embrace it because they knew who I was, but really they had no clue who I was. It takes more than name recognition to succeed. I learned that the hard way. Britney's career was built by an unstoppable machine, a team of experts with endless resources and a clear vision. In the hip-hop world, success isn't handed to you. It's earned. It's grassroots. You build an audience slowly, gaining respect and traction with every mixtape, every track. I didn't have that foundation. My first album was my introduction to the industry, but I never had the chance to grow into it. I went straight to the big leagues.

Signing a distribution deal through a William Morris subsidiary seemed like the right move at the time, but it ended up being another hard lesson. They were supposed to invest $250,000 into the project, which would've covered the tour and other expenses, but I never saw any of that money. I ended up covering the costs myself, nearly a million dollars of my own money. It was a real shock-and-awe eye-opener. One that taught me, at great expense, the importance of knowing exactly what you're signing up for.

CHAPTER THIRTEEN

T he way things ended between me and Britney—it was abrupt. But there were signs. Stuff I should've paid more attention to. Almost immediately after the album dropped, everything in my personal life unraveled. I was trying to juggle so much. Too much maybe. I went on a six-week promo tour for the album, but by the time I got back to L.A., my focus had to shift. The music had to take a backseat to the stuff happening at home.

It was the drinking while pregnant that tripped the first silent alarm in my head. And no, it wasn't heavy drinking, but it was still drinking. She was on medication at the same time. That mix was…dangerous. Fucked up, honestly. You're not supposed to drink when you're on meds like that. A couple of glasses of wine for her would hit like a whole bottle because of the medication. She was taking prescription pills and washing them down with half a bottle, if not more, of wine. I'm not saying she was pounding bottles every night, but it didn't take much to notice something wasn't right. But I kept making excuses. *She got thrown into the spotlight at sixteen. She's been dealing with insane pressure for years.*

And when you've spent so much of your life on tour, on the road for years at a time, how do you come back down to earth? How do you go from that level of pure adrenaline-pumped adulation and crowd-energy to just...being home? It's not easy.

Artists, musicians, there's nothing that compares to the rush of being on stage, performing in front of people. Whether it's a hundred people in a small venue or a packed stadium, the high of it is unmatched. And when it's gone, when the lights go out and the crowds are silent, that crash is brutal. I get it. So I went with that. The drinking, the meds, everything else—I kept telling myself it was just her way of coping, filling that void. I see it differently now. Those things weren't just little quirks or bad habits. They were signs, clear ones, and I just didn't want to admit it.

One of the biggest red flags had to do with my family, and how little we saw of them once the kids arrived. These were people who had always shown up for me. People who should've been there for every milestone with their grandkids. And yet, they barely got to visit. We had this massive house in Malibu: nine bedrooms, more than enough space. We could've had everyone out for a week or even a weekend, let them be a real part of the boys' lives. But that never happened. The only person who ever stayed overnight was her mom—and even that was rare. For everyone else—my parents, my siblings, even close friends—it was strictly day visits. A few hours, then back to a hotel or a red-eye flight home. And it wasn't because they didn't want to be there. It was because they weren't welcomed. That's when it hit me. This was more than just a phase. This was the life we were building. Or rather, the one we weren't. Slowly, I started to realize how much of myself I was pushing aside just to keep the peace. The only time I saw my boys, my closest friends, was when she was out of town or I could sneak away for a few hours. Everything else revolved around her world—her schedule, her moods, her rules.

The pressure just kept piling up.

It was like this slow build, one emotional brick after another. Meanwhile, I was pouring myself into my music—into that album. That was something just for me. A piece of me I could finally claim. I believed in it. I needed it. I was chasing this creative dream while also trying to hold it all together at home, and those two worlds were starting to pull me apart.

At the same time, Kori and Kaleb were still spending some weekends with my parents. Still having sleepovers at grandma and grandpa's, still making memories. My mom would fly out and spend time with them at Shar's house. They had that. And yeah, my parents would come visit me and Britney too, but always on a leash. No overnights. No "make yourself at home." In fact, there were times my family thought they were staying the night—bags packed, ready to settle in—and Britney would tell me they had to leave. And then I had to be the one to break the news. I had to be the bad guy.

That gutted me more than I ever let on. Because family means everything to me.

The life we were living wasn't what I imagined.

Not even close.

I'll never forget the day she fired the entire security team. I was in the studio, working on my music, when my boy Frank showed up to drop off an ounce of OG Kush, which wasn't so out of the ordinary. I liked to blaze, that's who I am, just to take the edge off. It had never been an issue before. But that day it was like something snapped.

I heard yelling outside in the courtyard, her voice raised, furious—and when I looked out, she was in Lonnie's face, screaming, "How the fuck could you let this happen?!" She was chewing out our whole security team. These weren't just employees. These were people we trusted with everything, the lives of our children. I'd known Lonnie for years. He'd been with us on tour, through every last ounce of madness. He was like family.

I stood there, stunned, watching this unfold, thinking: *What the hell is happening right now?* She knew I smoked weed. Everyone knew. My family, friends. I'd been smoking since I was thirteen years old. I'd even smoked with Britney a couple of times, so it wasn't like I was sneaking around or hiding anything. But now, suddenly, it was like I'd crossed some invisible line I didn't even know existed.

And then, just like that, she fired them.

All of them. Not just Lonnie. The whole team.

No discussion, no explanation, just gone.

I remember watching Lonnie stand there, stone-faced, trying to stay professional while she tore into him. I kept silently pleading: *Please don't grab her, man. Just walk away.* And he did, but you could see it in his face. It cut deep. It broke something in him, and honestly, it broke something in me, too.

After she stormed off, I pulled Lonnie aside, and I told him, "Don't worry, man. I've got you. You'll always have work with me." He wasn't a fan of touring, so I couldn't bring him on the road, but I made it clear that he was still part of my team. Same with Big Mike. These guys were my people, and I wasn't going to let her anger destroy what we'd built together.

But that wasn't the end of it.

After the blow-up outside, I went upstairs to cool off. That's when Britney came storming into the bedroom, holding Preston, and just ripped into me. Screaming. I stayed calm, trying to decipher what was really going on. I wasn't hiding anything. She knew who I was. She married me knowing it. But she was on the warpath, shouting her head off. Then she slapped me. Right in the face. With our son in her arms.

Preston burst into tears. He felt it. That dark energy. And in that moment, I knew I had to walk away. Not for me—for him. I didn't scream. I didn't retaliate. I just stepped away from the fire.

It wasn't really about the weed. That was just the excuse. The truth was, something deeper had shifted between us—respect, communication, trust. That slap was the first time things got physical. It wouldn't be the last, but that one stuck with me. Even after we split, she'd still bring it up. Still harp on the weed. But I never lied. Never changed. She married me knowing exactly who I was.

After that, the whole vibe in the house shifted. She hired a completely new team. One minute, we had a full staff we trusted— nannies, housekeepers, security. The next, we were surrounded by strangers—people I didn't know or trust, who didn't know our kids. And that matters. You don't just shrug that off. I couldn't rely on these people the way I had relied on Lonnie, Mike and the others.

That was when I started pulling back. Not from her, exactly, but from the situation. I didn't feel safe in my own space anymore. I felt like a stranger in my own house, surrounded by people I couldn't trust. And that's a terrible way to live, especially when you're trying to raise a family and build something stable.

Since then, I've replayed that day a thousand times, trying to make sense of it.

Maybe it had nothing to do with me at all. Maybe it was the pressure, the postpartum, the pregnancy—the weight of everything crashing down at once.

I don't know.

What I do know is this: *something broke that day.*

And we were never the same after.

CHAPTER FOURTEEN

M y album release party on October 31, 2006—
Halloween—was a day that I will never forget. I had
already shot a music video for my single in Las Vegas,
and with our son Jayden being born on September 12, there was
a lot of big life moments going on. Back then, albums typically
dropped on Tuesdays, and Halloween just happened to be one.
That night, everything seemed lined up. I was going through
all of the emotions leading up to the event: excited, nervous,
fucking anxious and feeling on top of the world at the same time.

Britney told me she wasn't planning to come out with me
that night. She said she'd stay home with the kids. Preston was
a little over a year old, and Jayden had just turned six weeks. I
understood. It didn't seem like she wanted to be out and about
and in crowds. She was only six weeks postpartum. I had a
packed schedule that day. It started early with appearances on a

few L.A. radio stations. My first stop was with Ryan Seacrest on his morning show, promoting his Halloween party for KISS-FM later that night in West Hollywood, where I performed before heading to the release party.

The party was held on a sound stage at Paramount Studios. I arrived with my boys, Eddie and Big Mike, my security at the time. Friends, family, and even some of Britney's relatives were there. They had their own VIP section roped off, so I hadn't seen them yet. Walking in, we took a back entrance up to my dressing room. Big Mike and Eddie were in front of me, leading the way up the stairs. As we reached the top, Jamie Spears, Britney's dad, was standing there. I hadn't expected to see him, so I was happy he'd decided to come support me. He threw a look my way, shook his head, and motioned to my dressing room door. His expression sat in that flat blank space between disapproval and apprehension, as if to say: "She's here, and it's not good." I was surprised because the last I heard from Britney earlier that day was that she wasn't coming.

Big Mike opened the door, and there they were: Britney, her brother Brian, Jason Trawick, her agent at the time, and an actress who was about to blow up from a role that would transform her life. They were sitting around the coffee table in my dressing room. The first thing I saw was Britney and her young starlet friend snorting a fat line of coke off the table. Both were wearing these outrageous wigs. Britney's was electric blue. It was surreal. They didn't even try to hide it. Eddie was right there with me.

Jamie, still outside, didn't see anything. He didn't want to know and wasn't sneaking any peeks. But he could sense something was up.

I was stunned.

Not because of the drugs. I've never been one to judge anyone for partying or letting loose. Hell, who doesn't like to keep the party going? But seeing her there, like that, at my album release party, just felt wrong. I wasn't even really tripping about the coke. I already knew she'd done it before, along with a whole bunch else. That wasn't the shock. What was hitting me in that moment was everything else, what this meant for the kids. Of course I wanted my wife to be at my album release party, but she told me she was going to stay home with the kids and I understood.

So then her whole group cleared out, including Britney. I remember she gave me a hug, tried to act like nothing happened. But she knew I wasn't happy. Everyone else just kind of muttered *hello* and got out of there as fast as they could. Britney could tell right away that the scene didn't sit right with me. Before she walked out, I asked who was watching the kids. She told me her mom was watching them, and I'm thinking: *Alright, cool.* But deep down, something felt off. I could tell she's wired, probably from a mix of whatever she'd been doing and the drinks she was still throwing back.

She left the room to find her friends and let me get ready.

Then, while I was getting dressed, she went downstairs and made a beeline for my parents. She was crying, telling them that I didn't love her anymore. Just throwing this whole scene at them, making it all about her.

I'm trying to play it cool, but in my head, it's just this loop: *We don't give the kids formula; you breastfeed them. Are you seriously going to go home after this and feed them like you don't have a body full of drugs?*

I had seen it before, her drinking and breastfeeding, and it was really upsetting because of the danger to the kids. I had already asked her to stop doing that. I wasn't upset that she was there; if she wanted to support me, I'd have been good with that. We could have prepared. She could have pumped milk for Jayden so her mom had that ready. But the way she was that night had nothing to do with us; it was something else entirely.

We were sitting at the booth, my family and friends all around, music blasting, people dancing. I was just sitting there, nursing my jack and coke, stuck in my own head. She was next to me, and I finally just leaned over and said it, quiet enough so no one else could hear, clear enough to make my point. I said: "Please don't go home and breastfeed the kids like this. Call your mom or someone. We need to get formula. You can't do this."

Man, the look she gave me. The instant rage in her eyes. Like she wanted to slap the shit out of me. Instead, she stood up, took her drink, and threw it straight into my face. In front of everyone. My family, my best friends, the whole damn table. I was in all-white. And she soaked me with a vodka cranberry. Then she stormed off with her crew, leaving me there, humiliated and pissed; but more than anything, worried.

103

First thing I did was call her mom. I was trying to stay calm, but I was frantic. I told her, "Do not let Britney breastfeed. She's been drinking and doing drugs." Her mom told me that Britney had been gone most of the day and that Jayden hadn't eaten for hours. Then I called security at the house and told them to get formula. Problem was, our boys had never been on formula. That's not an overnight switch. It's a process, and I was trying to manage all this while still at my own event.

People were asking if I'm going to perform, and I couldn't even think straight.

Will from the Black Eyed Peas came up, asking me if I'm good and I just shook my head, like: *I can't, man. Not tonight.* I was supposed to perform, but I couldn't, not at that moment. So the Peas got on stage and did their thing. My mind was spinning. This was supposed to be my night, and instead it was a disaster.

But at that moment, I didn't care about the drink in the face. I didn't care that she was doing coke. I cared about my kids. About her going home and potentially hurting them because she wasn't thinking straight. That's all that mattered to me. And that's when I knew…this was the beginning of the end.

That was the proverbial final straw, the breastfeeding thing. Her reaction. That's what ended us. Was that the only thing? Or was it all the little things piling up? I don't know, but in that moment, it was like the world collapsed.

Her mom called me, frantic, saying, "Kevin, Britney kicked me out of the house!" I was shocked. "What? What do you mean she kicked you out?" Her mom's voice was shaking. She said, "As soon as Britney got here, she started ranting and raving, and she told me to leave. Security made me get off the property."

I was sitting there, still at the after-hours spot, trying to process this mess. I mean, I was supposed to leave for New York the next day. Promo lined up—Hot 97, TRL, Webster Hall. It was all set. My album had just dropped, so this wasn't just a trip; this was *the* trip. But all I could think about was what the hell was going on back at home.

I left that party and headed to the Roosevelt Hotel.

Britney was supposed to meet me there. The plan was simple: we'd stay the night, then fly out to New York the next morning. All of us. The boys, her, me. Together. She was supposed to join me on this promo run. But none of that happened.

Instead, I called my lawyer, Mark Kaplan. Mark was the guy who handled our prenup before we got married, and I trusted him. I laid it all out for him—the breastfeeding, the erratic behavior, everything. I told him, "I need to figure out a way to stop her from breastfeeding my kids." I wasn't doing this to be cruel. I was scared. Terrified. I went to my lawyer because that night I realized that she was done listening to me reason with her. I had seen her do this many times before. Like when she fired our whole security team, or got rid of her longtime assistant Felicia (Fee) or canned her manager, Larry Rudolf. She was done hearing "no" from me. I felt this was the only way to get her attention and make it clear I was serious. Most people don't call their lawyer to draft a legal letter demanding that their wife stop breastfeeding their children while under the influence. But how do you get through to someone who won't listen to reason?

For me, it went well beyond one act. It was about trust. How could I trust her not to do worse behind my back? Throwing drinks, snorting coke, kicking her mom out of the house? It was like the floodgates had opened, and I couldn't close them. I couldn't unsee the possibility that my kids were in danger. Mark drafted the letter that day. It wasn't a divorce filing, not yet, but it was a line in the sand.

When I got to New York, everything was a blur. I wasn't in the right state of mind to deal with the press, but I had no choice. I had to go through the motions. I had invested too much time and money. I didn't want to be there, but I felt like I had to be. I smiled for the cameras, shook hands, did the interviews; but inside, I was wrecked. Every second I wasn't on stage or on air, I was thinking about her, about the boys, about what the hell was happening to my family.

I couldn't even bring myself to pick up her calls. She left voicemails—apologies, explanations—but I couldn't listen to them. I just couldn't. I was too angry, too hurt, too wrapped up in my own head. Then, as if I didn't already have enough, I got hit with this wave of guilt. She was trying to fix things, and I was shutting her out. But how do you move past something like this? How do you forgive someone when you don't know if you can trust them anymore?

What shook me the most was realizing how fragile everything was. If she could make a choice like that, breastfeeding our boys while high, what else was she capable of? And how many times had it happened before without me knowing? That was the moment it all became clear to me. The breastfeeding thing was just a symptom. This was part of a much greater pattern. The recklessness. The lack of accountability. And it wasn't just her. It was me, too. I had let things slide for too long, convinced myself everything would be okay. By the time I left New York, I knew things couldn't go back to how they were. Not after this. I didn't know what the future looked like, but I knew one thing for sure: I had to protect my kids, no matter what.

People around Britney liked to say, *It's her world, we're just living in it.* And for a while, I believed that. I believed we could make it work, that love would be enough to fix the issues. But love doesn't mean anything if there's no trust.

That week, everything changed.

The marriage, the family, the plans, it all started falling apart. And maybe it had to. Maybe that was the only way to wake up and see things for what they really were. This was the end. But it was also the beginning. Of something else. Something I didn't choose but had to face anyway.

After New York was Toronto for an appearance on MuchMusic, the Canadian answer to MTV. The show was their version of TRL, this huge live broadcast with screaming fans packed in the studio. Normally, I'd thrive on that energy. But this time, I was dragging myself there, already feeling drained from everything going on back home. It was almost a week since I had sent her the letter.

I got to the studio, went through the usual motions with producers, and prepped for the show. My mind was racing, but I told myself to lock it down. *Focus*, I kept thinking. *Get through this*. I mean, I knew what to expect, another day answering the same questions, until a producer ambushed me—right before I went live on air—with: "How do you feel about Britney filing for divorce?"

My brain just…froze.

I must've looked like a deer in headlights, staring at the guy like he'd just spoken in tongues. My first thought was, *What the fuck are you talking about?* Nobody had told me. Not her, not her team, not my team—nobody. That's how I found out. I just sat there, forcing myself to keep it together, trying not to let the world see me break. But inside, I was unraveling.

Then we go live, and the host starts in with the questions—about my music, the album, the promo tour. I'm hearing everything as if it's bouncing around an echo chamber. I'm talking about the tracks, my creative process, whatever; but my mind was stuck backstage. Did I just hear that right? Divorce?

You have to understand, up until that moment, I had no idea. None. I thought we were still figuring things out. Yeah, shit was tense. Yeah, I'd sent that lawyer letter about the breastfeeding thing. But divorce? And now, I'm trying to privately process this on live TV after being sucker-punched with the news. From the press, no less. Are you kidding me? That's worse than being served with divorce papers.

I wanted to get up and walk off that set right then and there, but I couldn't. The cameras were rolling. People were watching. The crew was standing around, oblivious to the bomb that had just been dropped on me. I had to sit there and act like I was fine, like my whole world hadn't just flipped upside down.

I couldn't even lock in exactly on what I'd said to the producer who'd ambushed me, some bullshit answer. Something vague, something noncommittal. I can't even remember. Probably something like, "Uh, yeah, I'm still processing everything," or, "It's a private matter." I don't know. Thank God my team had convinced the producers to stay away from mentioning it during the live broadcast.

The second the interview was over, I bolted. I didn't even wait for the wrap-up or the post-show meet-and-greet. I just grabbed my phone, called Mark Kaplan, my lawyer, and asked him, "Is this true? Is she really filing for divorce?"

It was. Mark confirmed it. He got a call from her lawyer just as she was walking into the courthouse to file the paperwork, but the press had already gotten a hold of it.

The timing of it all pulled the rug right out from under me.

It hadn't even been a full week since that crazy night at the album release party, when everything blew up with the breastfeeding drama. From me sending a letter about protecting my kids to her lawyer filing for divorce. It all happened so fast, I couldn't even catch my breath. At first, I wasn't even angry. I didn't get the chance. I was too busy being blindsided, too busy trying to figure out what this meant for me and the boys. This was much more than a breakup. It was a public unraveling of my life, right in the middle of my album release. Later, Britney claimed that she was legally advised to file for divorce before I got the chance. Her PR team thought that after the Timberlake breakup, it would look bad if she was on the receiving end again.

In that single week, I went from trying to fix my marriage to scrambling to figure out how to protect myself in a divorce. And yeah, it hurt like hell. But that one instant, sitting in that MuchMusic studio, emotionally concussed on live TV, was like a wake-up call. The end of my marriage. A whole new chapter. But a messier, uglier chapter than I ever could've imagined.

CHAPTER FIFTEEN

As soon as the interview finished, I stormed off the set and grabbed my phone. I called anyone and everyone who might know just what the hell was going on. Imagine, the mother of your kids files for divorce, and you're the last to find out. It was humiliating, infuriating, and devastating all at once.

Things weren't perfect. The honeymoon phase had ended, and we'd been fighting more lately, but I never thought it would come to this. Still, I should have seen the signs. One minute, she'd be laughing, and the next, she'd be screaming or crying. I never knew what to expect. Every day felt like walking on eggshells, and no matter what I did, it was never enough. The mood swings, the unpredictability, it was a lot. Like when she fired Big Mike and Lonnie over that weed thing. Or the attitude she copped when I caught her doing blow at my launch party. It was like: *Fuck you, I'll do whatever I want.* Defiance was her favorite gear.

The divorce side-swiped me. The first few days after she filed were a blur. No calls, no explanations, just silence. I was on my promo tour, jumping from city to city. The world was falling apart, but I couldn't. I had a schedule to keep, shows to do, interviews to give. But beneath the surface, I was a wreck. I felt lost and betrayed. I wasn't thinking about fixing things with her. That door slammed shut the second she filed. The worst part was I hadn't seen Preston and Jayden. My focus shifted entirely to them. I knew I had to stay in their lives, no matter what. And yeah, I was angry. I was furious about the way it all went down. Furious that Britney didn't even think about how it would affect me. Or the boys. But more than anything, I was scared. Scared for them, scared for what their future would look like. All I wanted was to hold them, to make sure they were okay. But I couldn't, not yet. I still had commitments to fulfill, and she had our sons and wasn't going to let me see them.

Soon after, I was constantly being bombarded with reminders of how far gone everything had gotten. I was getting late-night calls from her, drunk, with the sound of my kids crying in the background. It crushed me. There was one night, though, that really sticks with me. I was in Miami for work, trying to stay focused on my commitments, and I got a call. It was her, Paris Hilton, and Lindsay Lohan on the line, drunk as hell, begging me to come over. I could hear Preston and Jayden crying in the background. It had to be three or four in the morning. That call was the final straw. I'd already seen the photos in the tabloids, the ones of her out with them all night, partying at Paris's Malibu place. But hearing my kids crying while she was doing God-knows-what? That was it. Any deep-seated sliver of hope that I'd held onto, that we might still somehow pull it together for the kids, died right then.

It wasn't a one-time thing, either. It was all part of that reckless pattern. I kept coming across the same stories, the same pictures, the same behavior, over and over. She wasn't ready to change, and I couldn't keep waiting for her to figure it out. Every time I started doubting myself, every time it got hard, I replayed those calls in my head, the ones where she was drunk, the ones where I could hear Preston and Jayden crying. That was all the motivation I needed to stay the course.

So I put my head down and started preparing for the fight of my life—the fight to be their dad. Nothing else mattered anymore. Not the interviews, not the shows, not the headlines. It was all about them.

After I finished the press tour on the East Coast and wrapped up in Miami, I flew back to Los Angeles. It had now been about a month since she filed for divorce. I had no idea where she was, maybe New York, maybe somewhere else. All I knew was that I needed to figure out what came next. My stuff was still at the house, but I couldn't just walk in and grab it. Everything had to go through lawyers now. Every step I took had to be approved, signed off, and scheduled. Nothing was easy. Even though she was in L.A., she wouldn't let me see our sons. It'd been over a month since I'd last seen them. The only place I could see them was online or in the tabloids, being dragged from city to city while she was out partying all the time. I was speaking to Mark daily, desperately trying to get time with them.

For a couple of weeks, I was living out of a hotel while I tried to find a place to rent. Eventually, I found a house in Tarzana. It wasn't much, just a temporary spot while I searched for something more permanent, but it was big enough for me and the boys when I finally got them. All I cared about was making sure I had a space that felt like home for them. I was already planning what I'd need: cribs, toys, formula, everything to make sure they were comfortable when they came to stay with me. But that didn't happen right away.

It took months before I could see them. Jayden was just six weeks old when this all started, and Preston was barely over a year. They were babies. My babies. And I was stuck on the outside, trying to get a glimpse into their lives. I remember hearing stories about her going out, partying until five in the morning, leaving the kids with nannies she barely knew. That killed me.

When I got back to Los Angeles, my lawyer had to fight just to arrange a visit. I didn't see my boys for two, maybe three months. And when I finally did, it was only for a couple of hours, with her there, watching every move I made. It wasn't enough. It never was.

Those first few months were brutal. I was learning everything on the fly, how custody worked, how to fight for visitation rights. I had no idea what I was doing, but I knew one thing: I wasn't going to lose my sons. My first request was simple: they needed to be on formula. After what I'd seen, I couldn't trust that breastfeeding was safe for them. I don't know what her team told her; but eventually, the switch happened. That was the first win. A small one, but it mattered. I started getting my house ready, working with my lawyer to set up proper visitation. I wanted joint custody—50/50, no less. That was my line. I wasn't going to let her take them from me.

At the same time, I was unraveling.

The divorce, the fight for the kids, the media scrutiny—it was eating me alive. I started going out more, drinking more, slipping up and doing coke now and then, anything to drown out all the chaff and escape the weight crushing me.

No matter how dark things got, I kept pushing.

Preston and Jayden were my anchor. Every move I made, every fight with my lawyer, every sleepless night in that empty house in Tarzana, it was all for them. I was building a home for them, a safe space where they could be kids, out of the line of fire. I still don't know how I held it together. Maybe I didn't. But what I do know is that I never stopped fighting.

Even when the marriage tanked, it didn't make it any easier to watch her spiral. I loved her, and seeing her go through all that pain, even if mostly self-inflicted, was hard. She was the mother of my boys. No matter what happened between us, I never wanted anything bad for her. But the partying, the erratic behavior, the constant hiring and firing of people, it was like watching someone slowly lose control of their life. That's when the guilt kicked in. I kept questioning myself: Am I doing the right thing? Am I really giving my kids the best shot at a normal life? I'd go back and forth in my head, trying to justify it; but deep down, I knew I was making the right call. I had to believe that.

I remember thinking: *This isn't just about me anymore.* It wasn't about whether I was hurt or angry or heartbroken. For the first time in a long time, I had clarity. I started to see what life would look like for Preston and Jayden if Britney and I had stayed together—constant conflict, instability, a battle over every decision that could harm them. I wasn't raised that way. My parents were far from perfect; but they always put us first, especially after their divorce. They taught me what it means to be a parent, even if they didn't realize it. I wanted that for my kids. Stability. Security. A chance at a normal life. And over time, I realized that staying with her, trying to make it work, would never have given them that. It was a hard truth to face, but it was the best possible outcome. It wasn't even about whether I still had feelings for her, which, let's be real, I did. It was about our boys. About giving them a shot at a better life than the one they'd have if I'd stayed. But knowing that didn't make it any easier. Watching her struggle, knowing she was still the person I'd fallen for once, but also knowing that staying with her wasn't an option. It tore me up. It put me in this dark, depressed state where I felt like no matter what I did, I was losing something.

That's the thing about love—it never just disappears. Even when it's over, even when you know you're doing the right thing, it still hurts. I hated seeing her go through it, but I hated even more what it could mean for our kids. I couldn't sit by and let that become their reality. In the end, I had to let go—for them and for myself. It wasn't easy, and it sure as hell wasn't pretty. But it was necessary. And if I had to do it all over again, I wouldn't change a thing. All that mattered was giving our boys the best shot at life.

Before it all came undone, there was this moment when I thought maybe, just maybe, things could turn around. It came out of nowhere: a call from her mom, telling me to get to the Beverly Hills Hotel. Fast. She said there was going to be an intervention, and I needed to pick up Preston and Jayden. I didn't know what was going on, but the urgency in her voice told me it was serious. I could tell she was frightened—frightened for her daughter and what was happening in her life. She said they needed me to take the boys because they weren't sure how things would go. I didn't ask questions. I just went. When I got to the hotel, they were all in the same suite from the first night we met. The moment I walked in, I could feel the weight in the room. It was quiet, but not in a peaceful way. There was this deep, somber energy, like everyone was bracing for something.

Her family had already started talking to her, trying to convince her to go to rehab. I wasn't part of the initial conversation;

but when I walked in, I could see how serious everything was. She'd been crying, and everyone around her looked worn down, like this had been building for a long time. It wasn't angry or confrontational. It was sad. There was love in that room; but it was shadowed with fear—fear that she wouldn't agree to get help, fear of what might happen if she didn't.

When it was time for me to take Preston and Jayden, she came up to me, and we hugged. I'll never forget that moment. She was crying, and I could see she was scared—of losing everything, that her life was slipping out of control. I tried to reassure her. "It's okay," I told her. "I'm not taking the kids away from you. This is the best thing you can do right now. I'll bring the boys to see you. Just tell me when, and we'll make it happen." I meant it. The last thing I ever wanted was for her to feel like she was losing her babies forever. That wasn't what this was about. This was about giving her a chance to heal, to regroup. And making sure the boys were safe while she figured things out.

As much as I wanted to believe this could be the turning point, the reality was already clear to me. Her lawyers had tried to downplay things, claiming it was just an Adderall prescription issue. But I'd seen too much to believe that. The late nights, the partying, the photos splashed across every tabloid. Her family knew it, too. Everyone in that room knew she needed help, and this intervention was their way of trying to save her.

When I left the hotel with Preston and Jayden, I felt a mix of emotions. Relief that they were safe with me. Sadness for what she was going through. And hope that this would be the moment that changed everything. She hugged them goodbye, and I could see how much it hurt her. It wasn't easy for any of us. Driving home, I kept telling myself this was the right thing to do. They were too young to understand what was happening, but I could see the confusion in their little faces. It broke my heart, but I had to focus on the fact that they were okay now.

At the time, I was twenty-eight, still figuring out how to navigate all this. But I knew one thing: my kids came first. No matter how much I cared for her, no matter how much I wanted her to get better, I couldn't let anything jeopardize their safety. It was that day at the Beverly Hills Hotel when I realized, loving someone isn't always enough. Sometimes, you have to let them go so they can help themselves. And as hard as it was, I held onto hope that she'd take this opportunity to get better.

CHAPTER SIXTEEN

I had just settled into the house I was renting in Tarzana. My mom was there helping with Preston and Jayden. Jenny, my amazing new nanny, and Big Mike were around too, keeping an eye on things. Everything felt like it was starting to settle, at least as much as it could after everything we'd been through.

Then we got the call.

Britney's security reached out to mine and told them she had checked herself out of rehab and was headed to my house. They also warned us. It wasn't looking good. Big Mike immediately went outside, pulled the SUV up to the front door, popped the back hatch of the Denali, and sat there waiting. My house was gated, with a large wooden gate that opened remotely onto the driveway. Britney pulled up with a swarm of paparazzi on her tail.

She showed up at the gate, ringing the bell and shouting a bunch of things that didn't make sense. The only words that came through clearly were: LET. ME. IN. Over and over again. Then she started climbing the front gate and Big Mike had to stop her.

I couldn't even process what I was witnessing. My first instinct was to protect the kids. I told my mom and Jenny to take them upstairs. They didn't need to see her like that, not in this state. They'd already been through so much, and this would have been too much for them to handle.

I stayed inside with the kids, trying to keep things calm. I couldn't stand to see her like this. When Big Mike came back, he told me she was displaying erratic behavior, to put it mildly, not in her right mind: talking gibberish. I told him I heard her. Obviously, she was in no condition to be around our kids. Mike had turned her away. It was the right thing to do. I couldn't let her see them. They wouldn't have understood why their mom was looking and acting so bizarrely, and I didn't want to scare them.

What made it worse was that her showing up like this brought the paparazzi right to my front door. Up until that point, they hadn't known where I was living, but now they did. Suddenly, there were photographers climbing fences, snapping pictures through the windows. The house didn't even have curtains or blinds yet. I was scrambling to hang sheets over the windows just to block them. It was out of control. And it didn't stop there.

After Big Mike turned her away, she went down to some random hair salon in the neighborhood. When the stunned stylist turned her down, Britney took matters into her own hands, grabbing an electric clipper and shaving her own head. Eventually, she drove down the street to a gas station. That's where things escalated, the infamous "umbrella incident"—when she grabbed an umbrella and started swinging it at the paparazzi. They were having a field day. The photos from that moment wound up everywhere—her shaved head, the wild look in her eyes. That was the exact energy she brought to my gate earlier. Seeing those photos later, I thought: *This is what I was dealing with.*

It's hard to even explain how surreal it all was. It felt like something out of a bad dream. I was torn between so many emotions. Shock at seeing her like this. Fear for what it all meant for our kids. I kept thinking: *What is going on? How did it get to this point?* This wasn't the person I knew, the person I'd married. She was a completely different version of herself, and it was soul-wrenching to see.

But as much as I cared about her and wanted to help her, I couldn't risk letting her see the boys in that condition. My priority had to be their safety and well-being. I wasn't trying to punish her. I just couldn't put our kids in that situation. No matter how much it hurt to turn her away, no matter how much it broke my heart to see her like that, I had to focus on them. I didn't have all the answers, but I knew one thing for certain: our boys needed stability, and it was up to me to give it to them.

That night marked the first time I realized just how far things had spiraled out of control. I thought it couldn't get any worse.

I was so wrong.

A year later, Lonnie was handling the exchanges with Britney, taking the boys to her house and picking them up when it was time to bring them back to me. It was one of those scheduled visits, the kind we'd done countless times. Lonnie—my guy, my security, my family—handled the drop-off just like always. The boys were supposed to spend the afternoon with her, and he'd return later that evening to bring them home.

That day, my nanny Jenny had written a note for Britney's nanny, just a little heads-up about Jayden's eczema and his allergies. Poor kid had it bad behind his knees. He was allergic to all kinds of stuff: dogs, shellfish, certain fabrics. Jenny just wanted to make sure they knew how to take care of him while he was over there, because it kept happening when he'd come back from her house. She wrote everything down, and Lonnie handed that note off when he dropped them off. Britney wasn't even there yet. She was at a deposition for our custody battle. But Lonnie left the boys with her nanny like we always did, thinking it was just another smooth exchange.

Hours later, Lonnie went back to pick them up.

That's when it all went sideways.

Britney's nanny met him at the door, gave him Preston, and told him Britney had locked herself in the bathroom with Jayden. She was refusing to hand him over. Saying all this wild shit, that Jayden was being abused at my house. Total bullshit.

Lonnie called me right away. I remember feeling totally winded, like the air had been knocked out of my lungs. I could barely breathe. I can't even describe the fear and helplessness I felt in that moment. Jayden was just a baby, barely a year old, and he was locked in a bathroom with his mother, who wasn't in her right mind. Immediately, I called my lawyer, Mark Kaplan, asking what the hell I was supposed to do. This wasn't some minor family argument; this was court-ordered custody. Britney didn't have the right to keep him. I had to figure out how to enforce that without turning it into a scene. But it was already too late for that.

Someone called the police.

Lonnie's sitting in the car with Preston, who, thank God, had fallen asleep and didn't see any of what was about to happen. Hours went by. Hours. We just sat there, helpless, waiting. The street outside her house started filling up. Cops, ambulances, reporters. I had my assistant go grab Preston and bring him back home so he didn't have to sit in that mess.

Lonnie stayed behind, just waiting. I kept blowing up his phone, demanding updates, barely able to keep it together. I was pacing the house, losing my mind. What started as a custody pickup gone wrong had blown up into a full-on standoff. And my son was locked in the middle of it.

When they finally got her out of that bathroom, it was dark outside. They brought her out on a gurney, strapped down, wearing a damn straitjacket. The image of her being wheeled out like that, completely out of it, haunted me. She was incoherent, clutching Jayden, refusing to let go. The police had to pry him from her arms.

From there, Lonnie told me they weren't releasing Jayden to him, that they were taking him to Cedars-Sinai to get checked out and that I needed to meet him there. I didn't even hesitate. I grabbed Big Mike, and we jumped in the car and flew out of Tarzana like we were on fire. I knew that drive all too well. Jayden was born at Cedars, so it felt like déjà vu, but now in the worst possible way.

We pulled up and got in through one of the back entrances. When we finally got inside, they had Jayden in a little room in the ER. I could see him sitting there, looking so small, and my heart just shattered. The doctors were checking him out, trying to figure out if there was any truth to what Britney had told them. Of course, we'd already explained it was eczema on his leg. They're doctors, so it was clear to them what it was.

Finally, they cleared him. I scooped him up in my arms and got the hell out of there before anyone noticed. We made it back to my house, probably around midnight or one in the morning. Preston was already asleep, but it wasn't over.

Shortly after we got back, I had to wake Preston up, literally pull him out of bed in the middle of the night, because now they wanted to check him too. I remember having to strip him down to nothing but his little pull-up so they could check him over at the house. All because Britney had made these outlandish claims.

It was one of the hardest nights of my life.

I felt sick over what she was going through. This was someone I had loved. Someone I had built a life with. The mother of my children. And now she was being placed on a 5150 hold—an involuntary psychiatric detention for individuals deemed a danger to themselves or others. It was the first of two such holds that month. I'd never witnessed anything like it. How do you even begin to process that? All I knew was that I had to stay strong for my kids, even though I was barely holding it together myself.

Jayden was quiet for days afterward. You could see it in his little face. He didn't know how to process what had happened. Preston, who had already started growing anxious about visiting Britney's house, became even more hesitant. I tried calling her family, hoping for answers, but no one really knew what was going on. When someone is taken in like that, even close family can end up shut out. The doctors take over, and everyone else is left in the dark.

I'll never forget how it felt, watching everything fall apart, trying to pick up the pieces, and not knowing if I'd ever be able to put it all back together.

The day after Britney was placed on psychiatric hold, Mark, my lawyer, filed for emergency sole custody, requesting that it be granted until she got her life sorted out. It was the only logical thing to do. So much had already happened time and time again up to this point. Even then, the request wasn't permanent. It was intended as a temporary solution to protect our kids while she got the help she needed. But it wasn't a quick process. The custody battle had already been going on for a while, with countless hearings and endless scrutiny from the media. It was like living in the middle of a three-ring circus—paparazzi, journalists, helicopters tracking us all the way from home to downtown L.A. It wasn't just twenty guys with cameras anymore. It was a global spectacle.

Journalists from every outlet you could think of were camped outside, waiting to get a shot or a quote. And in the middle of all that craziness, we were fighting for the most important thing in my life: our sons. After the divorce was finalized, we moved straight into the custody phase. I wanted 50/50 custody. That's all. Equal time with our boys. I wasn't trying to take them away from her; I wanted to ensure they had stability in their lives with both parents. But she filed for full custody, and there was no way in hell I was going to let that happen.

Anytime you go to court, it's nerve-wracking. That's the one thing I learned from the experience; whether it was the custody battle, the divorce, or whatever else. I remember going on the stand just once during the custody case. I only had to answer a couple of simple questions, but it was intense. Being grilled by lawyers in a private boardroom during a deposition was one thing. It was exhausting and relentless, but not public. Getting on the stand, though, feeling like the whole world's watching, everything that mattered on the line, was a whole different ballgame. I remember my hands shaking the entire time, even though the questions were straightforward. It's a uniquely gut-wrenching experience, especially when you're fighting against someone you once loved so deeply, someone you thought you'd spend the rest of your life with—it's crushing. The last thing I wanted was to tear her down, to point out every mistake, every flaw, every incident. But I had to. I was fighting for my children.

California courts usually lean toward 50/50 custody in cases, and that would have been my preference, equal time for both of us with our boys, but the circumstances at the time made that impossible. The judge realized that a shared custody arrangement wasn't going to work, not while things remained this unstable. It was a heavy situation, and even though I wasn't initially fighting for sole custody, the court placed it on me. They saw that this was the best way to ensure Preston and Jayden's well-being. That did little to blunt the emotional trauma. The legal battle, the public scrutiny, and the sheer weight of the responsibility, it all felt like a whirlwind.

The courtroom was besieged with reporters. The judge would close the doors to the public as soon as the proceedings began, but still, details spilled into headlines. It felt like our personal lives were on display for the world to judge. And if the shit-show outside wasn't enough, she brought it into the proceedings. One day, she showed up in a wedding dress, the same one she wore the night we got married. It was bizarre.

But that wasn't the worst of it.

Another time, she delayed the entire proceeding by driving around the building for an hour while everyone, including the judge, lawyers, and even her own team, waited inside. It was not only frustrating, but disrespectful to all involved, especially the judge. And then there was the sheriff's deputy incident. She ran over a fucking deputy's foot with her car as she was trying to navigate the mob outside the courthouse. The poor woman had to go to the hospital. It was a big deal. The sheriffs were there for crowd control, to protect us from the rambunctious mob outside, and she made their jobs even harder. Those headline-worthy moments told only part of the story, though. There was a consistent pattern of her showing up late, creating scenes, and being disruptive. She'd arrive looking disheveled or inappropriately dressed, her demeanor erratic.

Every time she stepped into that courtroom, it felt like a performance. But this wasn't a show. The stakes were real. The judge kept trying to give her the benefit of the doubt. Her actions made that harder each time. This went beyond anything I said or the evidence submitted to the court. Her behavior painted a picture of someone unstable and unable to prioritize what mattered most: our kids. The judge couldn't ignore the difference: I came in prepared, focused on the boys. She was making headlines for all the wrong reasons.

The night she locked herself in the bathroom with Jayden and ended up under a 5150 hold was the tipping point. Combined with everything else—the wedding dress, the tardiness, the disruptive behavior—it became clear that she wasn't in a place to handle the responsibilities of custody. For me, it was painful to watch. This wasn't the person I'd fallen in love with, the person I'd built a family with. It was someone spiraling, someone struggling to hold it together. In the end, her actions spoke louder than anything I could have said under oath. And while it was heartbreaking to see her like that, it gave me the clarity to fight for what was best for Preston and Jayden. When it came time for the judge to make a ruling, I laid everything out. I was honest about what I'd seen, what I'd heard, and what I was worried about. I didn't drag her through the mud. I just told the truth, and that was enough. The judge granted me sole legal custody. That meant I made all the major decisions for our kids—medical, educational, everything that mattered.

CHAPTER SEVENTEEN

After the divorce, my life split into two distinct realities. On one side, I was a father fighting to give my kids stability, navigating a custody battle, and trying to make sure they had everything they needed. On the other side, I was young, newly single, and living a lifestyle that pulled me into a whirlwind of partying. Balancing those two worlds was challenging to say the least.

Dan, my manager, was one of the constants during that time. He'd been my manager when Britney and I were together, and when she fired him after the divorce, I decided to keep him on. I trusted him. He wasn't just some guy handling my career. He knew my situation, the mess I was in, and the stakes I was facing. He genuinely wanted to help me find a way to move forward. Whether it was figuring out how to keep my album on track or trying to create opportunities that allowed me to stay closer to home for the boys, Dan had my back.

But I wasn't exactly making his job easy.

When I didn't have the kids, I was out. Not "a few drinks with the boys" kind of out. This was a full-blown bacchanal bender of a first-rate Hollywood order, a journey through the underbelly of L.A.: strippers blowing cocaine in each other's asses, guys tag-teaming chicks in my hot tub, a bordello masquerading as a porn studio masquerading as a dental office…don't even get me started. I was young. Freshly single. Flashing my fame a bit. I was living in extremes: a responsible, devoted dad one day, a reckless party animal the next. I was having fun. But the truth was, I just wanted to numb the stress.

No matter what, my crew remained my grounding force. Jimmy, Marty, Eddie, Big Mike—they've always been my guys. Back then, and even now, they were the constants in a world that felt like it was spinning out of control. We'd hit the same spots, roll into the same clubs, and for better or worse, they were always there. My circle hasn't changed much over the years; definitely expanded a bit, but those core friendships have stayed solid. If there's one thing I'm grateful for from that time, it's that I had those guys with me, no matter how crazy things got.

And things got crazy.

Club appearances, event bookings—parties, parties, and more parties.

I was pulling in stupid money just to show up and party. A hundred grand to do Vegas or Miami, invitations to the biggest events, and trips to places I never imagined I'd ever visit. I was riding the wave of this strange sudden fame. 2007 was probably the most topsy-turvy year of my life. Here I am in the middle of the biggest shitstorm I'd ever been through—divorce, custody battle, the media ripping me apart—and meanwhile, I'm booking some of the coolest gigs I've ever had. It was like one minute I'm fighting for my kids, and the next I'm living out a dream.

One of those dreams became reality when I got asked to do a Super Bowl commercial for Nationwide Insurance. At first, the idea didn't really sit well with me. The whole concept was about making fun of myself as an artist. I'll be honest: I didn't love the idea of playing to the "bad guy" image that had been following me around. But then I suddenly realized that I needed to sit down, listen to the adults in the room, and trust that they knew what they were talking about. And let me tell you, they knew exactly what they were doing.

The commercial was genius.

I'm decked out like this over-the-top rapper, rocking a fur coat, sitting next to a stack of gold bars, a Ferrari parked behind me. I'm rapping about living large, and then, out of nowhere, someone yells in the background. The scene cuts, and suddenly, I'm in a fast-food joint flipping fries. The tagline was "Life comes at you fast." Even after we shot it, though, I was still harboring doubts. Everyone was telling me how great it was going to be, how it would change the narrative. Show a little humility and humor, they said. But I still wasn't sold.

Then came Super Bowl Sunday, and everything clicked.

The commercial aired and it was a huge hit—hilarious, sharp, and exactly what it needed to be. It allowed me to poke fun at myself in the smartest way possible. Everyone loved it. Seeing it land, seeing people's reactions, it was money. The people who'd pushed me into it weren't just hyping it up. They knew. They were right, and I finally saw how important it was to lean into the humor, to own the story instead of letting it own me. It was much more than just a commercial; it changed how I approached everything. I even got to go to the game.

What an experience, flying into Miami during Super Bowl week, right in the middle of all the madness: nonstop press, sit-down interviews, and for the first time, real media training. I needed it. Badly. I'd always been terrible at speaking. I failed speech class in high school. So learning how to control interviews, stay on message, and not ramble was long overdue. Nationwide put me up in a hotel, but it was way too exposed. One of our boys found a penthouse off Ocean Drive: rooftop jacuzzi, open floor plan, full deck overlooking the strip. We called it Casa de Fed. Miami was a madhouse that week, wall-to-wall people, Super Bowl energy everywhere you turned.

Nationwide gave me three tickets to their suite. I took Big Mike and my lawyer Mark. Still owe my dad for that one. He's always wanted to go to the Super Bowl, but Mark had been helping me through everything. And Mark being from the southside of Chicago, and a die-hard Bears fan, I couldn't say no. Before the game, Eddie hit me up—he was on tour with Justin Timberlake—and said, "I'm coming out tonight. Got someone I want you to meet." That's how I linked up with Jay Anderson, a beat facilitator to many, and a guy who worked with Fergie and the Black Eyed Peas. We hit it off right away. Jay and Fergie were in the suite next to ours at the game, and we started talking about Snoop's party at Mansion later that night. He said he'd make sure we'd hang with Snoop, and I was stoked.

Mansion was packed when we got there. I had one of the front booths right up against the stage. Roman Jones, a good friend of mine, always looked out. Same goes for David Grutman, Gino, Mo, Purple, Lyndon, Navin, Chris Jones (sorry, had to give my guys a quick shoutout). These are the dudes who run Miami's nightlife. The hospitality there is on another level, which is why it's always been one of my favorite places to visit. I've got so many great memories thanks to that crew. Mansion was Roman's baby, and any time I was in town, he made sure we were taken care of.

That night, he really came through.

I had Eddie, Big Mike, and even brought my lawyer, Mark Kaplan, out with us. I remember asking Mark if I should be worried about blazing with Snoop if the opportunity came up. He didn't miss a beat, just sipped his Platinum Patron neat and said, "Kevin, as your attorney, if you get the opportunity to smoke with Snoop Dogg and you don't, then you're a fucking idiot." Coolest lawyer on the planet.

Not long after Snoop started his set, he spotted me, cut the music, and said, "Fatherhood! My man K-Fizzle gotta be one of the biggest pimps in the world. Did y'all see that Super Bowl commercial?" Then my boy Jay grabbed me and pulled me up on stage. I walked over to Snoop, pulled a fat blunt out of my pocket, and handed it to him. He lit it right there and got back on the mic: "Ooooweee! Fatherhood brought the fire! This that real Cali OG shit!" The crowd erupted. For a kid who grew up idolizing Snoop—my nickname back in Fresno was "Snoop"—it was one of those memories that stays with you forever.

After the set, we rolled upstairs to Snoop's green room with Snoop, Jay, Daz, Kurupt, Magic Don, the whole crew. We had a couple drinks and were just choppin' it up. Meanwhile, another good friend of mine, Scott Storch, who's had my back since day one, hit me about the after-afterparty. I told Snoop and he was like, "Yeah, we'll see you up there?" It was five a.m., but in Miami that means nothing. Purple grabs a stretched Hummer and we pile in with at least forty girls. No exaggeration.

Scott's mansion? Unreal. A seventy-five-foot yacht docked out back. A bar inside that looked like it belonged in a Vegas club—thirty feet long, custom-lit. And underneath it? Enough weed and party favors to keep a small country high for a week.

I pulled up to the place flexing hard: forty-plus girls, me, Big Mike, Eddie, and my lawyer. It was way over the top. But really, it was all my boy Purple. He looked at me, smiling like, yeah, yeah, you know. And I just shook my head and said, "Bro, you're a fool for this." I love him for that shit, though.

Eventually, I made my way to Scott's office. When I walked in, he was on the couch with a glacier-sized mountain of coke piled on a gold tray on the coffee table in front of him. Snoop was sitting behind him at the desk. Jay and I sank into the lounge chairs across from them. A few minutes later, Mike Epps walked in.

The whole scene looked like something straight out of *Scarface.*

We posted up there for hours, Snoop rolling blunt after blunt, Scott hitting the extracurriculars, everyone cracking up, talking about the R&G album Snoop had just dropped.

At one point, Scott looked over and asked if we wanted any coke. Mike Epps turned to him and said, "Man, fuck you, Scott. Last time I did that shit with you, I was blowing black boogers out my nose for a week!" Like something straight out of his standup show.

We lost it. Couldn't breathe from laughing so hard.

That night, that whole week, it felt like the universe aligned. I'd gone from second-guessing myself, to a successful Super Bowl commercial, getting shouted out by Snoop Dogg, and then blazing with him and the homies till sunrise.

That same year I got invited to the Kentucky Derby. Talk about landing on another planet. The Derby's all about upscale elegance and tradition, a sea of famous faces, everyone dressed to the nines. They had seating arrangements for the prestigious Brown Family Gala and wouldn't you know it, I was at the table with the Manning family and a bunch of Colts players. Peyton, Eli and their wives were amazing people.

Next thing I know, they're the ones asking to take a picture with me. Eli Manning. NFL legend. And his wife's telling me he's a fan. Let that sink in. I had just watched in person as Peyton earned his first Super Bowl ring leading the Colts over the Bears. I remember thinking: *How does this even make sense?* Two of the greatest QBs ever, and one of them is acting like meeting me was on his bucket list.

Years later, I saw a clip where Eli was asked if he'd ever been starstruck. His answer? Meeting me. I still laugh about it because it's so nuts, but it also makes me think about how strange and unpredictable life can be.

You're my boy, Eli. You got that Tom Brady kryptonite and they can never take that away. Sorry, but I've always wanted to say that.

Later that night, I partied with Kid Rock at a club where my boy DJ Vice was spinning. I went hard. Maybe too hard, because the next day, I barely made it to the main race. Missed the whole day. Safe to say, I didn't get an invitation to return the next year, but I was truly honored for the invitation and the experience. It was weird trying to figure out how to live in this new reality, exhilarating and exhausting all at once. I didn't always make the right choices, and I know there were times when I let myself get swept up in the excitement.

WWE had also reached out to me. They were doing a show at the Staples Center in L.A. and asked if I'd come do a bit with John Cena. At first, I thought: *Why not?* I was promoting my album and WWE fans are some of the most passionate, wild, and loyal fans out there. It felt like a no-brainer. The plan was simple: I'd come out, play the villain, talk some trash, and Cena would take me down. They told me they'd use my single, *America's Most Hated*, as my theme song. I'd come out to the music, rile up the crowd, and Cena would interrupt and set me straight. Playing "the heel," the bad guy, was perfect, especially with the way people were viewing me at the time. The WWE thrives on drama, larger-than-life characters, and people you love to hate, and I was already getting plenty of practice at that in the media. Wrestling fans absolutely loved to boo and harass me, and I was happy to give them exactly what they wanted. Walking into the Staples Center that night, hearing the crowd erupt in contempt and vitriol, was electrifying. They despised me, and I loved every second of it. The instant I started walking down that ramp, I felt like I was born for it. The crowd went wild, hissing, jeering, screaming. I grabbed the mic, hyped myself up, and started trash-talking the crowd. Then Cena came out, and the place absolutely exploded. He grabbed the mic and started ripping into me, saying things about Britney, the tabloids, and everything else that made it personal. The crowd ate it up. Then he grabbed me, and the next thing I knew, I was in the air and slammed into the mat with his signature F-U. The place came unglued.

What I didn't realize going in is that there was no real training for that first night. They just told me, "Don't land on your neck." That's it. I had no idea how it would feel. So, I took a couple of shots of Jack backstage to calm my nerves and went out there. After Cena slammed me, I was sore as hell, but the adrenaline and the crowd kept me going.

The fan reaction was bigger than any of us expected. Vince McMahon saw something in the chemistry between me and Cena, and after the match, he pulled me and my manager aside. He said, "We need to do more of this." At first, I didn't know if I could commit, but when he laid out the idea of doing a full storyline that would build up to a pay-per-view match, I was in. It was a golden opportunity to promote myself, my music, and to have some fun. What had started as a one-off turned into a running feud between me and one of the biggest names in the history of the WWE.

Once I agreed, they brought me to their training facility in Venice. That's when I got a whole new level of respect for what these guys do. Wrestling is brutal on the body. After just a couple of days training, I was wrecked. Bruised and battered in places I didn't even know existed.

The storyline with Cena grew from there. I was teamed up with Johnny Nitro, his girlfriend Melina, and Umaga. I'd talk trash, slap Cena, and throw cheap shots, playing the ultimate cowardly villain to properly grandiose effect. At our big pay-per-view event in Miami, the crowd was fired up. Before I went out, one of the funniest things of the night happened. Backstage, I ran into Shaquille O'Neal and his kids. I asked the kids if they were ready to see me smash John Cena, and Shaq laughed and said, "Nah, we're here to watch Cena kick your ass." We both laughed, all in good fun, and it got me hype right before the show. Cena and I went head-to-head, and thanks to my team's interference, I actually won the match. Umaga came out, took Cena down, and I pinned him. The crowd unleashed a wave of boos. I celebrated, pulling wads of cash from my pockets and making it rain over Cena as he lay unconscious in the ring. The audience lost their minds. That's what made the WWE magic feel so real to me, drawing heat as the villain, feeding off the crowd, and just enjoying the ride. What a blast.

But Cena wasn't done with me that night. I was commentating on another match and Cena returned to the ring. This time, he wasn't holding back. He took out Johnny Nitro, Umaga, and everyone else, then turned his attention to me. He slammed me again with the F-U. The crowd went crazy, and just when I thought it was over, he picked me up and slammed me again. By the third slam, I was barely holding it together. One landing hit me flat along the side and knocked the wind out of me. It was brutal, but the crowd was loving it. I loved it, too. It gave me an escape, a chance to step into a role and embrace the opportunity rather than hide from it. For a few hours, I was just a villain in the ring, giving the crowd what they came to see. And man, those fans are loyal. They remember everything, and their energy is unmatched. Wrestling is a world all its own, and I feel fortunate to have played a part in it, even for a little while.

What made it all so surreal was that I was doing some of the greatest shit in my life while dealing with the worst, hitting the highest highs while living the lowest lows. I'd be in court one day, fighting to see my kids, and the next day I'd be shooting a Super Bowl commercial or stepping into the ring with John Cena. I think that's what kept me going, the work. Even when everything else was falling apart, life kept finding ways to remind me that it could still be good. And let's face it: I needed the dough.

CHAPTER EIGHTEEN

When your life falls under the spotlight, money has a way of becoming the center of conversation. Of course, Britney and I had a prenup, but it was a pretty standard one. There was no "I want X amount if we split" clause or anything like that, because honestly, when we got married, I didn't give a shit about the money or any of that legal stuff. I was head over heels in love, and completely consumed by what we had together. I wasn't trying to make demands or secure some big payday if things went south. I didn't see an end in sight. My lawyer, Mark Kaplan, tried to warn me. He'd seen it all before and knew how quickly things could change. But I was young, naive, and stubborn.

I thought: *That ain't never gonna happen to us—we're meant for each other.*

I really believed it, too. I think we both did. It felt like drafting up legal documents was just another box to check before we got back to building what we thought would be a forever kind of love.

When Britney and I divorced, the court awarded me $20,000 a month in child support. At the same time, I was receiving alimony, another $20,000 a month, for half the duration of our marriage. A marriage that lasted two years and change. People hear figures like that and think you're financially set. But the reality is far from that. Raising two young boys in Los Angeles, while maintaining the security and stability they needed, came with a price tag that would make anyone's head spin. The money didn't stretch as far as you'd think.

Take my house in Tarzana, for example. Just maintaining a home and a lifestyle that matched what the boys were used to with their mother easily ran well over $40,000 a month. Rent, security, a full-time nanny, transportation, and all the other day-to-day needs of raising two kids in L.A., as well as my two children with Shar—it added up fast. That money was gone almost as soon as it came in.

People love to assume that I was just coasting off her money, but that couldn't be further from the truth. Contrary to the tabloid headlines, I wasn't some bum just sitting around waiting for a check. I was out there hustling, grinding, investing—working to build a solid foundation for myself and my kids. My Super Bowl commercial alone paid almost a million dollars for just three days' work. It was one of the biggest paychecks of my life, and it felt huge. Not just for the money, but for what it represented, stepping out from under the shadow of my marriage as my own man. I was also stacking up appearances, getting $100,000 to show up at clubs in places like Vegas and Miami. I was hosting events, going to high-profile parties, and doing everything I could to keep my momentum going. At my peak, I was making $300,000 to over half a million a year, and it went much further back then. And with all that overhead, that cash spent fast.

I was still out there hustling, trying to earn a living, make a name for myself. Whether it was appearances, gigs, or new projects, I wasn't sitting idle. In 2008, I was offered a reality show with VH1 that could've set me up financially for life. The deal was almost done. Contracts were drawn, the terms were agreed. VH1 had promised the kids wouldn't be shown on camera. They'd either be off screen completely or shot from behind. That was the only way I'd even consider it. I wasn't going to use my kids for ratings. But at the eleventh hour, they came back and said they wanted the boys on camera, full face, or the deal was off. I didn't hesitate. I walked. No amount of money was worth putting my kids in the spotlight like that. I knew what that world could do to people, and I wasn't about to throw my sons into it just to cash a check.

I remember Mark, my lawyer, giving me some solid advice after the divorce settlement. He said, "Take a million dollars and put it somewhere safe where it can grow. You'll want that later."

But twenty-eight year old me thought I didn't need to worry about that. I figured I'd make another million in no time. I thought I'd keep doing appearances, booking gigs, and living the life. But that's the thing about being young—you feel invincible and think the money will never stop. Sure, I made some smart moves, like dumping a half-million into the house we bought in Malibu. By the time we sold it in 2008, my portion had more than doubled. I walked away with over a million dollars from that deal. But I also made plenty of mistakes, thinking that the lifestyle I was living could go on forever. The money was good at the time, but behind those numbers was a desperate dad doing whatever it took to give his kids a sense of normalcy in an abnormal world. And for me, that was worth every penny.

CHAPTER NINETEEN

ritney had her own unique perspective on things. She saw the events in her life through a prism that painted her as the victim, the misunderstood one, the person wronged by everyone around her. But from where I stood, she needed help. Whether that was rehab or therapy, I couldn't say for sure.

Whatever the case, it was clear she was in no state to responsibly manage her own affairs. She needed some form of oversight. A protective layer. When I first heard the word "conservatorship," I had little to no idea what that even meant. My lawyer had to explain it to me, and Jamie gave me his take on why it was necessary. The courts had granted him control over almost every aspect of her life—career, finances, medical decisions—to act as a barrier against further harm. It didn't take a genius to see that things weren't going well before this happened. The idea was to create some stability and ensure Britney had the structure she needed to concentrate on rebuilding her life and her relationship with our boys. At the time, I was relieved. I truly believed it was the right move for everyone involved.

Once Jamie took over, everything seemed to calm down. I was never involved in the conservatorship meetings or decisions about her career, and didn't want to be. That was all Jamie's domain. It seemed like he had a firm grip on the situation; and frankly, I wouldn't feel comfortable being part of that. But I supported the decision because I believed it was the only way to stabilize her situation, and more importantly, provide a safer environment for our kids. My only concern was Preston and Jayden. Too much had already happened for me to take any chances. Even after the conservatorship began, the judge insisted on having a court-appointed monitor present during her visits with the boys. It wasn't punishment. It was protection. I knew it would be hard for her, but the risks were too high. Her behavior had been erratic, and I couldn't let that jeopardize our children's well-being. The boys were young. Jayden was still a baby, and Preston was barely a toddler. I wanted to be sure they were safe. She'd see them for a couple of hours a few days a week under the watchful eye of the monitor, but no overnights. It was important to rebuild trust and create a situation where I felt comfortable letting her have more time with them. Slowly, over the course of months, we worked on it, step by step. It wasn't ideal, but it was necessary. As time went on, the visits got longer, and eventually, we built up to her having the boys overnight. It was a gradual process, but it felt like progress.

By that point, Jamie had really taken control of the situation. I found myself working with him on everything related to the boys. It wasn't what I'd ever imagined, co-parenting with someone's father, but it became the norm. Jamie was heavily involved, managing her schedules and helping her transition into a place where she could take on more responsibility with the boys.

For a while, it felt like things were moving in the right direction. Eventually, the court-appointed monitor was no longer necessary. Britney was having the boys for overnights at least once or twice a week. From what I could see, she was improving. She seemed more present, more engaged with them. I was relieved to see that. At the time, I thought, *Okay, maybe this is exactly what she needed.* There was still a long road ahead, and trust wasn't something that could be rebuilt overnight. But I let myself hope that maybe we were turning a corner, that maybe she was finding her way back to being the mom our children needed. For the first time in a while, it felt like we were finding a new normal. Her progress was uneven, but at least it was moving in the right direction. I wanted to believe she was finally stabilizing, but even then, challenges kept popping up—some small, some more concerning. She went through several nannies before finding one who could handle both her and the boys. Some of the people they hired couldn't deal with the stress or the environment. I heard later about lawsuits being filed by former employees, claims being settled quietly to avoid court. It was a mess I wasn't even fully aware of at the time. All I knew was that I wanted the boys to be secure, and if that meant dealing with Jamie and the conservatorship to make sure things were handled properly, then that's what I was going to do.

Around that time, she started working on music again. I'm pretty sure it was her decision, though with her, it was always hard to tell. One day she'd want to dive back into work, and the next, she wouldn't. I don't know if Jamie or the team around her was encouraging her to stay busy as a way of keeping her on track, or if it was just her way of finding a sense of purpose again. Either way, it seemed to be working.

In those early days, the conservatorship felt like a lifeline. It brought a level of order that had been missing for years. At the time, I thought Jamie's hard-nosed approach was exactly what Britney needed. He wasn't the type to sugarcoat things, and given how out of control her life had become, structure was critical. My focus was on making sure the boys had a safe space to visit their mom and that she had a chance to get back on her feet. Jamie's role seemed like a means to an end, a way to bring some much-needed balance to a fucked-up situation.

No matter what issues she was dealing with, those boys deserved better. They deserved parents who put them first. And as much as I wanted to believe she could turn things around, over time it became clear that her inability to see the harm she was causing made it impossible to hope. It was like hitting a wall over and over again, knowing it wasn't going to move.

I didn't want to be in this position. I didn't want to be the one drawing lines and making demands. But someone had to. Someone had to put the boys first, and if it wasn't going to be her, it had to be me. That responsibility weighed on me every single day. But I'd carry that weight a thousand times over if it meant protecting them from the fallout of choices they didn't make and couldn't control. Because there's no preparing for the kind of heartbreak that comes when your child clings to you like their life depends on it. Every time Preston had to go to his mom's, they had to pry him off my neck. He'd cry, scream, and hold on with everything he had. At night, he was the same. Jayden could sleep fine, but Preston wouldn't rest unless I was right there. Even the slightest movement would wake him in a panic. I'd sit beside his bed, my finger resting on his arm, and the second I moved, he'd jolt awake, crying for me. This wasn't a phase. It was fear, something too big for his little heart to carry.

For nearly two years, the cycle repeated. Night after night, he'd wake up terrified. No matter how deep his sleep seemed, if I let go, he knew. I realized I couldn't fix this alone. He needed help. A therapist quickly confirmed what I already feared: this wasn't just separation anxiety. Preston was showing signs of early trauma, even as a toddler. He couldn't explain it, but his actions spoke for him. He didn't feel safe at his mom's. Preston felt neglected while Jayden received most of her attention. Even as babies, it was obvious. One day, out of nowhere, he walked up to Jayden and bit him in the chest. Not out of random aggression, but frustration and jealousy. He saw what everyone else saw. His mom favored Jayden. I don't doubt she loved them both, but her actions made it clear who came first. Preston felt it, even before he had the words to say so. How do you explain to a two-year-old that his mom doesn't love him the same way she loves his brother?

I tried to make up for it, giving him the extra attention he needed, but some wounds run too deep, and there is no replacement for a mother's love. My nanny, Jenny, was a godsend. She came into our lives when everything was falling apart, and she immediately saw what the boys were going through. In her fifties, from Barbados, Jenny had this steady, nurturing way about her—her accent soothing, her patience endless. She understood the dysfunction they were experiencing and did everything she could to give them a sense of security. But even Jenny had her limits.

Once, I asked her to accompany the boys to their mom's house, thinking it might help. She went once, maybe twice, before coming back shaken. "Please don't ever ask me to do that again," she told me. She didn't explain fully, but she didn't have to. She had seen what I had, things no child should be exposed to. She stayed, but only in my home, where she could help care for the boys in a safe environment.

Preston carried that pain for years. The night terrors, the need for constant reassurance, the feeling that he wasn't loved as much as his brother—it lingered. Even as he got older and could articulate his feelings, the scars remained. Watching your child hurt like that is the hardest thing as a parent. You want to fix it, to take it all away, but some things can't be undone. All I could do was love him, support him, and make sure he knew, without a doubt, that I would never let go. This whole period was filled with lawsuits, rumors, and unsettling stories that, over the years, I've tried to piece together. They were stories that seemed too wild to be true, yet given everything else, I couldn't entirely dismiss them. One lawsuit that stuck with me involved Fernando Flores, a security guard who worked for Britney when the boys were toddlers. At the time, I didn't think much of it. The guy was claiming all kinds of crazy stuff, things that sounded like a cash grab, and I didn't argue with it. I was still locked in protect-the-family mode; the last thing I wanted was to feed the media beast.

Flores's lawsuit included a long list of disturbing claims. He said Britney exposed herself to him multiple times, walked around naked, made sexually inappropriate comments, and would intentionally drop things and ask him to pick them up while she was undressed. Maybe that stuff sounded tabloid-worthy, but one allegation hit differently—that she'd fed shellfish to Preston and Jayden knowing they were allergic. I know it happened. Because this wasn't the first time. It had happened before. Multiple times.

Not just with shellfish. She blatantly disregarded the fact that Jayden had serious allergies.

Publicly, I dismissed the whole thing. My lawyer even made a statement saying the lawsuit was frivolous. Everyone around me thought it was a shakedown. But years later, when the boys began talking about their own memories, the discomfort they felt, and how certain things in their accounts mirrored what this guy was saying, I had to stop and reconsider. Flores also mentioned neglect: leaving the kids unsupervised, hygiene issues, hitting them with a belt, unpredictable shouting. DCFS looked into it and didn't find cause to intervene, so I trusted that at the time. I wanted to trust that. But now, seeing the long-term emotional toll on the boys, I believe there may have been more truth in those allegations than I was willing to admit.

The case ended in a confidential settlement. No apology, no denial, just a quiet payoff. If it was all lies, why not fight it? Why not clear your name? Preston was just three or four when all this happened, still forming memories, and yet those years were already loaded with trauma. Hearing Preston and Jayden later talk about what they saw and went through brought me right back to that lawsuit. And it changed how I saw everything.

There were other smaller things, too—things that might seem trivial but, over time, spoke volumes. Jayden was kept on a pacifier far longer than he should have been, and when I finally got Britney to stop giving it to him, it felt like pulling teeth. She also kept putting Jayden in diapers long after he'd been potty-trained. When the boys started school, Britney would insist on doing all their homework, even after being told not to. It might sound minor, but it fits into a bigger dynamic of control and the denial of their independence.

Some incidents were far more serious. Once, while in Louisiana, Jayden was hospitalized. They told me it was an allergic reaction, but I later found out he had gotten hold of some pills. Whether they were Britney's or someone else's, I'll never know. Jayden also had severe allergies to horses, yet she would keep taking him riding despite knowing the risks. Even as a teenager, she tried to get him to ride, and I had to step in again. Food allergies were a recurring issue, too. She continued feeding Jayden shellfish even after knowing he was allergic, brushing off concerns like it wasn't a big deal. It became an ongoing battle just to ensure the boys' safety in situations where it should have been second nature.

Then there were the stories the boys shared as they got older. Preston once told me she had punched him in the face. I used to do every interview back then with a smile, keeping things light— always saying "we're doing great," always protecting her. But maybe that was a mistake. Maybe the truth needed to come out. Because covering it up didn't help her, and it definitely didn't help the boys. And the hardest thing to admit now is that the truth was always there, staring me in the face, and I didn't want to see it.

I felt like I was the only one truly looking out for them. I know that's not entirely true. Jamie loves the boys, and I know Britney loves them too. But love doesn't erase the trauma they endured or the bad decisions that affected their lives. And there's no telling how much more happened that I don't even know about.

The conservatorship brought stability when it was desperately needed, but it came at a cost for everyone. And I understand why people questioned it. It's easy to judge when you're not living it. But the cycle hasn't stopped. It's been the same highs and lows, year after year. Jamie Spears took on the role because he believed it was the only way to save his daughter's life. In the beginning I could see the fear and emotional toll that the situation caused him and her family. As a parent, I couldn't imagine how devastating it must've been for him and Lynne. As an ex-husband, I can't imagine how difficult it was for Britney to be under the control of her father as an adult. Maybe things would've gone smoother if Jamie had handed off the conservatorship to a professional much earlier. But I'm not going to get into what ifs or conspiracy theories. Jamie took on an impossible task, and in doing so, gave Britney a real chance to rebuild her relationship with our sons. He also tried his best to balance her physical and mental well-being, all while giving her some room to make some of her own choices. If she wanted to work then he would support it as long as she knew there was no backing out once the contracts are signed because the repercussions of breaking those agreements could have bankrupted her. If she wanted to take the boys on vacation to Hawaii or go to Disneyland or a basketball game, he worked with me to make it happen. We also made sure that she was involved in important decisions regarding our sons, even though I didn't have to. I wanted to make sure she knew she still had a voice when it came to our children. Everyone—and I mean everyone—was doing everything they could to bring things back to something resembling normal. Something safe.

Unfortunately, as time passed, getting back to normal no longer felt possible. Around the same time, the fans, along with the Free Britney media movement, were making their voices heard. They went after Jamie and anyone else who had played a role in her life. I tried to understand where they were coming from, but I could never fully get behind it. There were too many conspiracy theories, too many wild misunderstandings.

The Free Britney movement seemed focused more on Britney the pop icon—"Free our queen!" I used to hear all the time—than the actual person behind the fame. At times, it felt more like a fandom's mob mentality than genuine concern for Britney's well-being. But the movement kept growing, until it became a force to be reckoned with.

Honestly, I believe the pressure from the Free Britney movement led the judge to ignore the professional reports and cave to public opinion, especially with her own election on the line. But none of that truly mattered in the end. If Britney believed she was being held against her will, and everything else she's shared since, then that trauma is real for her. And you can't ignore that.

I've lost faith that things will ever fully turn around, but I still hope that Britney can find peace. Whatever her future holds, I hope it's one where she can finally take control of her own life, on her own terms. This whole saga, twenty years of it, was built on denial. Britney never reached the first step of recovery: admitting there was a problem. Not then, not now, not ever. And without that, nothing could truly change. Not the conservatorship, not Jamie stepping in, not anyone else. If you don't think you need help, you'll never accept it. From the bathroom incident with Jayden to reckless choices like partying when she was supposed to be parenting, it was always someone else's fault. She didn't think she had a drug problem. She didn't think there was anything wrong with the decisions she made. That refusal to take responsibility is the root of everything that's gone wrong.

The environment she was in didn't help either. When you're a star, especially at her level, it's easy to surround yourself with people who never say no. She had a whole entourage of "yes"-people, and I think that's why she valued me for as long as she did. I was one of the few people who would tell her no. I wasn't there to be her fan or her cheerleader. I was her husband and the father of her children. But that dynamic was unsustainable. People don't like being told no, especially when they're used to being told they can do whatever they want. But she was grounded, present. No sign of the madness to come. I knew she had done all kinds of drugs before, but she hadn't ever really gone off the rails until the night I caught her doing coke at my launch party.

It felt like the floodgates had opened, and everything started to unravel.

I mean, hey, I get it. Addiction and mental health issues don't just appear out of nowhere. They build up, sometimes slowly, sometimes fast, and when they hit, they hit hard. For her, it was like flipping a switch. The person I thought I knew was gone, replaced by someone I barely recognized. And as much as I tried to understand, it didn't change the fact that her choices, no matter what the reason for them, were affecting our kids.

CHAPTER TWENTY

Victoria—"Vic"—came into my life at a time when I felt like everything was spinning out of control. It had been two years since the divorce, and between work, raising my four kids, and trying to navigate Britney's world, I was having trouble just finding enough room to breathe. We met at a barbecue I was hosting at my house, sometime in late summer of 2008. As a running joke, when people ask how we met, I'd tell them I found her in my backyard one day. Back then, when the boys were with their mom, I partied a lot, but this was one of the more chill days.

My house in Tarzana was a constant hub: friends, security guys, the nanny. It had a big, beautiful backyard with a pool, a raised hot tub at the center, and the green of the tenth hole of the golf course stretching out in the background. There was a sitting area by a fireplace and a bar with a bench instead of barstools, something I thought looked cool but wasn't very practical. The barbecue was in full swing when Christina, a friend who came around once in a while, arrived with Vic.

I was sitting at the bar, talking with my brother Chris. The moment Vic walked in, she caught my attention. She was gorgeous, but it was much more than that. She had this undeniable pull about her that just drew me in—magnetic. We clicked instantly. She was from Washington State, near Pendleton, Oregon, which sparked a connection since my mom had lived there. She had played pro volleyball and worked at Fox Sports, which impressed me. More than that, unlike most people in my orbit, she was completely herself, down-to-earth, truly centered. The more we talked, the more I realized how different she was. She wasn't trying to be anyone, and that honesty was refreshing.

At one point, while sitting on the bench near the bar, Vic tried to stand on it, and the whole thing tipped over. She fell into a barrel roll, saving herself from face-planting, but couldn't save herself from the embarrassment. Chris and I couldn't help but laugh and assured her that it wasn't her fault because the bench was cursed. It lightened the mood, and we kept talking, but something really stuck with me. We were both a couple drinks in, and we ended up hanging out near this little outdoor fireplace. There was a coffee table out there, surrounded by seating, and we both had our drinks resting on it. At some point, Vic went to grab her glass, and it slipped, hit the ground and shattered. Glass everywhere. She looked at me, wide-eyed. "Oh my gosh, I'm so sorry," she kept saying. She felt awful. And I don't know, maybe she was nervous, maybe it was just one of those clumsy slips, but I remember just looking at her, like, who cares?

And then I grabbed my glass, looked her dead in the eye, and slid it off the table, smashing it down next to hers. Glass on glass. Like, now it's even. She tells everyone that's when I had her. Not just because of what I did, but because of what it meant. I wasn't mad. I wasn't weird about it. It was just a small gesture to say "Don't sweat the small shit. We're good." That simple act said a lot more than either of us realized. And the truth is, my friends could tell right away that something was different. I hadn't acted like that in a long time.

As the night went on, we just sat there by the outdoor fireplace continuing our conversation. By the time we stopped, it was five in the morning. She had to go to work without any sleep. Nothing had happened between us except for a kiss. We started seeing each other a short time after that. Vic wasn't like anyone else I'd met. She wasn't caught up in the lifestyle or looking to play games. She had her own values and stuck to them, which made me respect her even more. She wasn't in a rush to jump into anything, and that steady pace felt right. After years of instability and heartbreak, she brought something different into my life, something real and grounded. I didn't know it at the time, but that barbecue marked the beginning of a relationship that would change everything for me. Vic became the ringleader of my friends, no exaggeration. The way she stepped into my world, made it her own, and never asked me to shrink any part of myself, I'd never experienced anything like that. She isn't just someone I love, she's my best friend.

I'll never forget the first time Vic met Britney. I wasn't even there. Vic had never seen her in person. Not during the tour, not during all the times we were following Britney around with the kids. So this was the first time. And it was wild. Vic was outside in the front yard with the boys and our nanny, Jenny. This was back in Chatsworth, in a guard-gated community where I thought we had at least some level of privacy. Vic was playing with Preston, just a fun, normal afternoon, when they both looked up and saw Britney driving down the street. No warning. No heads-up. Nothing.

To this day, I don't know how she even got past the guards. Apparently, she pulled up to the shack and just started yelling until they let her in, straight-up bulldozed her way through with pure volume. Next thing they know, Britney parks, walks right up to the front door, and comes in like she owns the place.

She was wearing a corset top and Daisy Dukes so short that Vic could see everything. No underwear. One boob hanging out of a ripped shirt. In one hand she's got a single purple diaper. For Jayden. Who hadn't worn a diaper in over a year.

Jenny and Vic immediately took the boys inside. Preston bee-lined it to the basement to hide. Britney walked in, grabbed Jayden, sat him on the couch, and started undressing him. No hello. No "nice to meet you." Just stripped off his pants and tried to put that diaper on him like he was still one year old. Meanwhile, Vic, seeing all of this for the very first time, is just standing there in shock.

Then Britney heads upstairs. Jenny tried to stop her, told her she had no right to be there, but Britney ignored her like she didn't exist. Vic watched as she climbed the stairs, her ass and everything else just out in the open. She went straight into my bedroom, started opening drawers, digging through my stuff like she was casing the place. That's when Jenny went up there and let Britney have it.

Finally, she comes back downstairs without saying a word and leaves. Just like that.

When it was over, they looked at Jayden, still sitting on the couch in that purple diaper, with a confused look on his face, like, "Can someone please get this thing off me?" Preston wouldn't come out of hiding in the downstairs movie room until Jenny told him Britney was gone.

Vic told me later how surreal the whole experience was. It captured exactly what I'd been trying to prepare her for all along. I used to joke and tell her, "You've got problems," and she'd think I was talking about her. It wasn't until years later that I explained I'd been warning her about the whirlwind she'd stepped into by being with me. But Vic walked straight into that storm, and she didn't flinch.

That was her front-row seat to the full-fledged shit show.

And she stayed.

By then, Britney was finishing up an album and preparing to tour. Her dad Jamie was trying to figure out how to make it all work, knowing that I had full custody of the boys. She would be heartbroken to tour without them, and I wasn't letting them go without me. I had no intention of spending months away from my kids, and I was uncomfortable with them being on the road without a stable setup.

Jamie approached me with a plan.

I'd be on the road with the boys, staying in rented homes or accommodations near Britney's tour stops. Whenever she was close to where we were staying, she'd have time with the kids. It was structured so she'd never go more than a week without seeing them. On paper, it seemed logical, but looking back, I think it was a terrible idea. She should have learned how to sit still before being thrust into the pressure of a massive tour.

But the situation with the boys seemed to be improving. Preston, who'd struggled with anxiety and night terrors early on, was starting to grow out of that phase. Jayden was as easy-going as ever, and they both seemed to enjoy their time with her. From the outside looking in, everything appeared to be on the up and up. I felt like I was making the right decision by agreeing to the tour, even if it meant putting my own life on pause.

The decision wasn't without its challenges, especially when it came to my relationship with Vic. We'd only been together a few months when I told her about the tour. We had already developed a close bond, spending almost every day together, even though she lived in Long Beach and I was in Tarzana. When I broke the news that I'd be traveling for over a year, it was tough. I wanted her to come with me. She was becoming such a steady, positive force in my life, and I couldn't imagine being apart from her for that long.

Jamie, however, disagreed. He thought having Vic on the road would complicate things, arguing that it could affect Britney's state of mind. Initially, I agreed to leave her behind, and Vic stayed back while I hit the road with the boys. But as the days turned into weeks, it became clear to me that the situation was untenable. Vic was much more than a girlfriend; she was becoming my partner, someone I wanted by my side.

I remember calling Jamie to tell him I was bringing her out. He tried to convince me it wasn't the right time, but I couldn't let someone so important to me be sidelined. I'd already been through enough to recognize what mattered, and Vic mattered. She came out to join us when we hit New York, and even in the whirlwind of tour life, she fit in effortlessly. There was something about her energy—steady, calm, uplifting—that made everything seem a little less overwhelming.

She wasn't fazed by the chaos of my life. She simply adapted and became part of the family. What struck me most about Vic in those early days was her sense of self-worth. She wasn't like anyone I'd met before—firm in who she was, clear about what she wanted. She didn't fall into my life without boundaries or expectations. She valued herself, and she made me value her even more because of it. From the start, I felt like she was teaching me something about relationships, about trust, and about what it meant to truly care for someone. She didn't force anything; she let our connection grow naturally, and before I knew it, I couldn't imagine my life without her.

Despite everything she witnessed, Vic never faltered. She supported me through the madness, through the nights when I broke down from the weight of it all. She didn't just help me; she became a source of strength for the boys, too. She never tried to replace their mother or force a maternal role on them. She wanted to offer a safe place for them, someone they could turn to if they needed support. They call her Vic, not mom, and that was always her choice. She respected the complex dynamics of our family and found her place without stepping on anyone's toes. In many ways, she's been more of a mother to the boys than anyone else, but she's done it with grace and humility, always putting their needs first.

Vic's selflessness extended beyond our family. When we met, she was an accomplished athlete, a two-time All-American volleyball player and a rising star in the world of professional beach volleyball. She had a promising career ahead of her, with opportunities in sports broadcasting and endorsements. But she put all of that on hold to be with me. She won't admit it, but I know that being with me meant putting her own dreams on hold. It's one of the reasons we moved to Hawaii. She loves volleyball, and coaching at her alma mater has always been a dream. I want her to have the chance to chase that dream, just as she supported me in mine. Of all my relationships, nothing compares to what I have with Vic. She's taught me what it means to love and be loved, without conditions or expectations. Vic is the one I've been searching for my whole life, the one who made all the madness and mayhem of life make sense, and the one who finally gave me a reason to believe in forever.

CHAPTER TWENTY-ONE

B y the time I hit thirty-one in 2009, my life had taken a turn. I had let myself go and was out of shape. Touring, not dancing for years, and a general lack of focus on myself had caught up to me. I'd gained a ton of weight, topping 230 pounds. When *Celebrity Fit Club* came calling, offering a hefty paycheck for nine weeks of work, it felt like an opportunity to hit the reset button. They dangled close to half a million dollars for what was essentially a part-time gig just down the street from my house in Chatsworth. All I had to do was show up a couple of days a week and follow their program. Easy enough, or so I thought.

The experience, as it turned out, was anything but straightforward. Before the ink on my agreement was dry, I got a curveball: they'd brought my ex-girlfriend Shar onto the show. I knew reality TV thrived on drama, and the producers must have been salivating at the prospect of throwing us together. That's not who I am, though. I don't play into manufactured conflicts, and I had no intention of falling into that trap. It wasn't the drama I wanted; but for that kind of money, I figured I could keep my head down, avoid the theatrics, and just concentrate on following the fitness regimen.

Celebrity Fit Club wasn't just your run-of-the-mill weight-loss program. It had a boot camp vibe. Shot in Simi Valley, the show's set included obstacle courses, bungalows, and a drill instructor named Harvey, a no-nonsense military guy who woke everyone up at the crack of dawn to train, eat, and train some more. There was also a nutritionist and a doctor on hand, both of whom doubled as judges alongside Harvey. They gave us tailored meal plans, provided weekly challenges, and tracked our progress. It was like an amped-up version of *The Biggest Loser* but with celebrities.

Despite all the reality show nonsense, the program worked. I dropped close to forty pounds in nine weeks. They gave us prepped meals to take home for the four days we weren't on set, which helped me stick to the program. I didn't realize how much I missed feeling healthy until I started shedding the weight.

My confidence grew as the pounds fell off, but I also discovered something else: I hated reality TV. The producers, true to form, tried to stir up drama between Shar and me. At one point, they orchestrated a scene where I apologized to her on camera for how things had ended between us. The apology was sincere, but it felt forced in that setting. I realize now that I hadn't fully reflected on my behavior or what I owed her until much later in life. What aired on TV was a performance of closure rather than the real thing, but maybe everything I was going through was karma coming back to bite me in the ass.

The show's cast was a mix of personalities, including Bobby Brown and Sebastian Bach. Some of them fed off the drama, turning up the volume for the cameras. I didn't fault them. It's what the producers wanted. But it wasn't my style. I kept my head down, stayed out of the conflicts, and focused on the workouts. That's who I've always been: low-key, chill, not the guy who stirs the pot.

After *Celebrity Fit Club*, reality TV offers flooded in. Everything from *Big Brother* to *Wife Swap* landed on my desk. They even floated my name as a potential host for *Dancing with the Stars* when the show first started, but I turned it down. At the time, I couldn't see the appeal and couldn't have guessed how massive that show would become. In hindsight, I missed an opportunity there, but I've never been one to chase fame for fame's sake. I was also being offered massive amounts of money from media outlets to do the tell-all circuit. Cash in on the cache. We're talking six-figure deals that I was turning down for the sake of Britney and my family.

Reality TV wasn't all bad. It gave me a chance to prioritize my health, and the paycheck was hard to argue with. But it also opened my eyes to how manipulative the medium could be. The manufactured drama, the constant pressure to "turn it on" for the cameras, it just wasn't me. The experience left me wary of the industry just when reality TV was dominating pop culture.

Still, I walked away from *Celebrity Fit Club* with more than just a lighter frame. I learned that I could push myself, that I wasn't stuck in the unhealthy rut I'd fallen into. Not a life-changing epiphany, just a step in the right direction. I've never been the guy with a six-pack, and I wasn't trying to become one. But for those nine weeks, I proved to myself that I could make changes when I put my mind to it.

The show also reinforced something else: I needed to be selective about my choices moving forward. Not every opportunity is worth the cost, even if the paycheck is tempting.

Instead, I worked on finding projects that aligned with who I was, not who the world wanted me to be. I wasn't burned out, necessarily, but I was done chasing opportunities for the sake of it. For a while, I did little things here and there, but nothing significant. Preston and Jayden were entering grade school—kindergarten, then first grade—and their lives became my focus. It didn't make a conscious decision to step back; I just went with what felt right. They needed consistency, and I was the only parent who could provide it.

After *Fit Club*, the partying that had defined a big part of my twenties began to fade out of my life. Sure, I had a few wild nights here and there—trips to Vegas, nights out when I didn't have the boys—but it wasn't the same. It felt hollow. I started to realize that the lifestyle I'd been living didn't align with the person

I was becoming. Slowly but surely, it all came to a halt. I was growing up, stepping into the role of a father in a way I hadn't fully embraced before.

Work slowed down on its own, but I wasn't chasing it either. I'd still mess around with music here and there, but I wasn't trying to release anything. It wasn't for lack of material. I had some great songs, ones I was genuinely proud of. I worked with Grammy-winning producers and songwriters, building an album that felt like it could really make an impact. But I couldn't bring myself to put it out.

By that time, I could feel the weight of the responsibility on my shoulders. Britney's visits with the boys were frequent enough, but there was always something going on in her world: issues with her agent/boyfriend, Jason, clashes with her dad, or decisions that made me question what kind of environment the boys were walking into, like the time they came home with their hair bleached. Not just streaked or lightly done. It was bleached down to their scalps. Their skin was burned. I had to shave their heads, and their scalps looked like leopard print from the chemical burns.

Incidents like that drove home the reality that I couldn't trust things to be consistent or safe on her side. It wasn't malicious, just poor judgment. And the boys needed better than that. When they started school at Sierra Canyon, a private school, it solidified my resolve to put them first. From that point on, my life revolved around ensuring they had the stability they deserved.

The reality was clear: I couldn't chase a music career and be the father my boys needed. It wasn't even a hard decision. With everything going on in Britney's world—her tours, her career still in full swing—someone had to be the constant for Preston and Jayden. Whether the rumors I heard about her personal life were true, I couldn't gamble on their welfare. Even if just a fraction of what I was hearing was real, it was enough to make me step back and reassess everything.

Britney continued to work, putting out music, going on tour. I let the boys visit her a few times while she was touring, but it was nothing like the first tour. Back then, we were all constantly on the move for over a year and a half. It was too much for everyone. This time, I prioritized their schooling and routine. They'd visit her here and there, but the days of uprooting everything to follow her schedule were over.

For me, it was a choice between being a father or chasing dreams I'd been chasing for years. And there was no competition. My dreams could wait; my kids couldn't. Their childhood was happening right in front of me, and I wasn't going to miss it.

Sometimes, things felt okay, like some semblance of normalcy was within reach. The boys started playing sports—flag football, baseball, soccer. We'd show up to games, and Britney would be there. There are even pictures of us together, sitting on the sidelines, talking while the boys played. It wasn't perfect, but it wasn't a shit show either. She was still under the conservatorship, and Jamie was still running the show. At that time, things seemed stable enough for us to have those shared experiences as parents.

But beneath the surface, there was a lot I didn't know. Jamie would tell me years later, "You have no idea... You probably know maybe ten percent of what's gone on over the course of this thing." He's never gone into detail, and I've never pushed for answers.

Part of me doesn't want to know.

CHAPTER TWENTY-TWO

I remember walking into the house one day and Vic was upstairs in the bedroom, visibly shook. I went up, sat down beside her, and asked, "What's wrong?" She looked at me, took a breath, and said, "I'm pregnant."

"What?" I could see she was nervous. She didn't know how I was going to take it. But I just kind of looked at her and laughed. Like, "Babe, I've got four kids already. What kind of reaction do you think I'm gonna have? This is incredible!" Vic already meant the world to me. I had no doubts. I'd never had a relationship like this, and I wasn't going anywhere. So once she saw that, once it landed that we were in this together, the nerves faded, and it turned into what it should've been from the start—pure joy. We were getting ready to have baby number five. It felt wild, but it felt right.

The pregnancy went well, but that labor was grueling. Vic was determined to do everything naturally. No meds, no epidural. We even had a doula with us at the hospital.

Jordan came into the world like a little sumo wrestler—eight pounds and some change. Just perfect. Every time a new baby comes into your life, it feels completely new, no matter how many times you've been through it. It's familiar, but still unreal. And this time, it just felt complete. Like family. Her mom was there. My parents as well. Later, Preston and Jayden would come meet their little sister. That stuff means everything to me. A baby being born should be a family affair. That's the way I've always felt.

Not even an hour after Jordan was born, I got a call from my agent Nina. I picked up, and she's like, "Hey, you got a minute?" And I'm like, "Not really. I just had a baby." And she's like, "Congratulations, that's amazing, Shit, okay, quick, I got an offer for you."

It was another reality show. Another shot at a weight-loss journey, this time in Australia. It was called Excess Baggage. She started throwing numbers at me, and I'm sitting there like, holy shit, we just had a baby and now I've got a job offer that would soon take us across the world for five months.

As soon as I hung up, I went to Vic, wiped from labor, and told her, "I think we're moving to Australia." She threw me an exhausted look that said, "Please shut the fuck up." She couldn't even process it yet. But I couldn't help it. My adrenaline was off the charts. I had to say something.

Of course, the logistics immediately started weighing on me. The boys were in school, and we had 50/50 visitation. Britney was getting ready to go on a run in South America, and I knew we had to figure out how this would work. I talked with Jamie, and we worked it out: she'd take the boys while she was on tour, and Lynn would fly them out to me in Australia afterward so we could keep things balanced. Then I'd be back for Christmas and we'd split time again.

I handled all the passports and got everyone prepped for the move. We flew to Sydney, and I started filming. The show itself? Man, it was a mess. The concept was solid, the storylines were real, but the way it was put together was a total disaster. It flopped hard. They hooked us up with this insane penthouse in Neutral Bay. It sat on top of the hill, overlooking the bridge, the Opera House, the whole city of Sydney. It was unreal. We had our own rooftop pool, and that place became our home base. Vic was there with three-month-old Jordan, settling in, while I had to travel almost every other week to film. I didn't even have time to see the place before heading out. The show had me on the move non-stop, first to Melbourne, then to Perth, and then up to this remote-ass place two hours from a city called Kununurra, in the Kimberley region, Northern Territory. That's straight-up Outback. And not the steakhouse. We're talking the whole Crocodile Dundee vibe. At night, you'd shine a flashlight outside and see crocs floating right off the back patio. The place had deadly snakes, spiders, all of it. Closest hospital was two and a half hours away. I was loving it. I felt like I was walking through the same shit I used to watch glued to Nat Geo or Discovery Channel as a kid.

One night, around one a.m., it was 120 degrees and we were filming by the water. I started spinning. I didn't pass out, but I was fading—fast. I thought: I'm gonna fucking die out here in front of the whole cast and crew. I had this freaky sensation of the life being drained out of me. It felt like those dementors in Harry Potter, just pulling pieces of me out. They got me back to my room with the AC on full blast, gave me two IV bags. Still not coming round. That's when they rushed me the two and a half hours to the hospital.

The doc didn't wait. He had me pee in a cup. When only a couple drops came out, they immediately hit me with cold IV bags, one after the other. They didn't have time to get them to room temperature. That shit felt like needles stabbing through my heart, but it saved me. He said if I'd gotten there thirty minutes later, my kidneys could've failed.

I spent three days in that hospital recovering.

Technically, I lost weight fast, but it was the wrong kind of weight loss. Nearly dying isn't a diet. The silver lining was I got to see more of Australia than most Australians ever do. Tasmania, Gold Coast, Kangaroo Island, all of it. Eventually, Vic and Jordan joined me, and we got to experience it as a family.

But that trip wasn't without drama. I had a clash with Jamie over the kids. I called him like, "When are the boys flying out here?" and he hit me with, "They're not." I lost it. Screamed at him. He gave me the structure argument—school, stability, all that. And he told me, "You can take me to court." I was filming. I couldn't fly back and fight this. He knew that. Jamie and I have always been cool. I respect him, feel bad for him, honestly. But this wouldn't be the last time we butted heads when it came to what's best for the boys.

After we got back from Australia, I knew I hadn't gotten the weight loss results that I achieved during *Fit Club*. I didn't take it nearly as seriously, especially after being sick. I was still heavy, and it was obvious that it was getting to me. Vic saw it right away.

Next thing I know, she's out here reaching out to food companies—meal delivery, health stuff, whatever she could find. She finds this one—I think it was "The Fresh Diet"—and ends up locking me in for a deal. I don't remember the exact number, maybe $25K or $50K, but it was an endorsement deal to be on their program for a year. They delivered meals to the house, and I really committed to getting back in shape. Mirrors went up in the garage. I started dancing again, doing resistance and cardio work. I was shedding it.

And in my head, I knew why.

I was gonna propose to Vic. I wasn't thinking traditional. I didn't want to do the whole get-down-on-one-knee-in-a-restaurant thing. That just didn't feel like us. So instead, I planned the whole damn wedding first. No joke. I planned the wedding before I even asked her to marry me. I got one of the penthouses at the Hard Rock Hotel in Vegas. Back when it was still the Hard Rock. I brought in about forty of our closest family and friends. Me, Vic, her family, and Jordan. I made sure the boys stayed with their mom that weekend, which to this day, I do regret. I wish I had all of my children there. We got to the room, and once we were all settled in, I got everyone together. I had already asked her dad for his blessing. Her brothers, her mom, they were all in on it. I dropped down and proposed right there in front of everyone. Vic had no clue. She was shocked. Tears, hugs, the whole thing.

And while we were hugging, I told her she had forty-eight hours to get everything ready. We're getting married right here in two days. Vegas wedding. I had a wedding planner ready to go who came in and helped Vic with everything. We got married that Saturday, just a couple of days before Jordan's birthday. She was our ring bearer. Everything about that weekend was perfect, and I will cherish the memories forever.

Within six weeks, Vic was pregnant again. Peyton was coming. And we're still not even sure if she's a honeymoon baby or a wedding night baby, which would explain a lot, because she's our little firecracker.

When Peyton was born, she came out with these bright blue eyes, blonde hair, total spitting image of Vic. Jordan had a lot of me in her, but Peyton? That was all her mama. And it was awesome. Vic is obsessed with sports. Her two all-time favorite athletes are Michael Jordan and Peyton Manning. The instant we found out we were having kids, she was set. Girl, boy, it didn't matter. First baby was going to be named Jordan, and the second was going to be Peyton. Period. And she wasn't kidding. She told me straight up: "I don't care what anyone says. My kids are getting named after the greats."

Jordan and Peyton.

Two powerhouse little girls, each with their own fire.

As of 2014, I had a full six-pack—of kids. Three different moms. I remember being young, telling my parents I was gonna have seven or eight kids. They laughed it off. But damn, I came pretty close.

It didn't matter that they had different moms. All that mattered was making sure they were all connected, that they knew they had each other. That was the whole goal. I did everything I could to make that happen, driving hours in L.A. traffic to go pick up Kori and Kaleb, arranging trips, making sure they never missed time with their brothers and sisters. Shar lived far enough away that it wasn't easy, but I made it work. Because it mattered.

I've always believed that family isn't just something you're born into. It's something you build. And we were building it. Every time Preston and Jayden held their baby sisters, especially when Peyton was born, I remember seeing how proud they were. That look in their eyes, like, "This is my little sister." Nothing but pure love. I have the pictures of them holding her, but I don't need them to remember. I always will.

What meant the most to me was watching them all come together naturally. They weren't acting like half-siblings. There was no distance between them. They were just brothers and sisters. That's what we were creating. A real unit. A team.

And Vic was key in that.

She made it so no one—the boys, or Kori and Kaleb—ever felt like they were just visiting. This was the most important thing. My family. All of them. Not just the kids I was raising full-time. All six of them, together, knowing they could always count on one another. Because that's what I want most. When I'm not around, I want them to be able to call each other and know someone's gonna pick up. I want them to have each other's backs, no matter what.

That's what we were building. That's what everything has always been about. My children.

CHAPTER TWENTY-THREE

W hen I got back from the show in Australia, it hit me: I couldn't keep chasing work if it meant going months without seeing my kids. I told my agent Nina straight up: no more reality shows, none of that. If a commercial or something easy came up, fine. But I wasn't chasing gigs like that anymore. It wasn't worth it. I needed to be present.

We had moved back to Tarzana, into this smaller four-bedroom place. It was under 2,000 square feet. Not tiny, but with four kids, it felt tight. At least the neighborhood was decent, safe, but it definitely wasn't Calabasas. The space brought us closer together. The kids played with each other more, spent less time on video games. They were all into skating then, and we'd hit the skate park down the street a couple times a week. The girls were still really young, and their brothers loved doting on them. There are some really special memories from that time.

But while we poured ourselves into building a warm, loving home life, the boys were dealing with things I could no longer ignore. Preston was about ten or eleven when he came to me, asking why his mom kept forcing him to bathe with her. It was clear he was uncomfortable, to put it mildly, and I had to step in and make it stop.

By the time they were teenagers, the boys told me they didn't want to go to their mom's house anymore. At first, I chalked it up to typical teenage rebellion or minor spats. I'd reassure them, "It'll be fine. You've got people there looking out for you." The court mandated that they spend time with her, and I wanted to encourage that relationship. But they were insistent, and soon they showed me why.

Preston and Jayden recorded several incidents on their phones. One video showed Britney screaming at Preston over a shirt he didn't want to wear for a photo for her Instagram. He wanted to wear a blanket because it was freezing outside, but she demanded he put on the shirt. Jayden filmed the tail end of it: her yelling, Preston pushing back, and her temper exploding. Another video showed her in the car, berating Preston, calling him names, while turning to Jayden and speaking to him in baby-talk: "Why are you looking at me like that, baby? Are you okay?" The favoritism was glaringly bizarre, and it wasn't lost on Preston. He already struggled with feeling overlooked, and that sort of favoritism only deepened that wound.

Another video showed her barging into Jayden's room at midnight, waking him up to put lotion on his face when he had to be up for school by 6:30 the next day. He filmed her yelling about respect and going off on him like Joan Crawford on crack, while he protested, clearly tired and confused. This wasn't an isolated incident. She would regularly wake him up in the middle of the night and drag him to her room to keep her company or watch movies with her. This had gone on his whole life to that point, just one more thing that required my intervention to stop. It was a pattern: she'd pull him into her room at all hours, leaving Preston alone. The imbalance in her attention toward them was beyond frustrating—it was harmful.

Then came the stories that shook me to the core. The ones I didn't hear until the boys stopped seeing her. They would awaken sometimes at night to find her standing silently in the doorway, watching them sleep—"Oh, you're awake?"—with a knife in her hand. Then she'd turn around and pad off without explanation. Creepy as fuck. Other nights, they'd wake to the sound of her screaming bloody murder or smashing things in the house. All of this terrified them.

One night, after another unsettling visit, the boys came home and said, "We're done. We're not going back." By this time, they were thirteen or fourteen, old enough to make their feelings clear. Preston and Jayden said, "You can't make us go." That was the breaking point.

At first, I struggled to believe it. I thought maybe they were exaggerating or misinterpreting her actions. But as the stories piled up, and the videos corroborated their claims, the facts were impossible to ignore. I thought back to a prior conversation Jamie and I had. Jamie had told me they had taken all the knives out of the house and locked them in the security room. At the time, I thought this had something to do with her and her boyfriends. When I finally heard these things from the boys, I realized it directly involved them and that was never explained to me. Then I heard from someone on the inside who was worried about her. They told me what she had done to her cars. The leather seats in both vehicles—a $250,000 G-Wagon and an SL650—were all slashed up, with the knives still left inside. Apparently, she had a habit of stabbing the upholstery. The seats were destroyed. Hearing all this floored me.

Britney was due to start another Vegas residency. It was all set to kick off, with tickets already on sale and the dates announced. But then Jamie got hospitalized with a ruptured colon, something serious enough that he almost didn't make it. Shortly afterward, Britney canceled the Vegas shows. Officially, the reason was Jamie's health, but it was clear to me that she was also struggling mentally. The Vegas leg being called off felt more like an escape hatch for everyone involved. She didn't want to do it, and this provided a convenient excuse. Behind the scenes, though, it was clear Britney was on a downward spiral. Around that time, she was sent to this facility, and she was gone for weeks, maybe even a month or more. I don't know exactly what went on in there, but it's something Britney has spoken about publicly since the conservatorship ended. She's claimed that they locked her in a chair for hours at a time, kept her heavily medicated, and forced her to comply. She's shared those details on social media and even alluded to them in her book. I can't say how much of it is true, but it's clear that it has caused her a great deal of trauma, and when she came back, the tension between her and her family escalated to new heights.

That was also when Britney began using social media to unleash her frustrations, particularly toward her family. She called out her dad, her sister, her team, anyone she felt had wronged her.

Then Preston told me how a fan went after him online. This person, a Free Britney militant, was pressuring him to support his mom publicly. And in frustration, Preston told them things he'd experienced. He said she'd hit him, threatened him with a knife, acted violently and dangerously. He was only sixteen then, and I remember telling him not to air out personal stuff online. But that's what blew the lid off the knife situation, how I first learned about Britney's disturbing behavior. And it made me wonder how I'd missed it for so long. For years, I had been under the impression that things were stable enough, but then I realized as time went on that the damage was too deep to repair, and the situation was more complex and fractured than I'd realized.

This was around the time COVID hit, and everything went into lockdown. There were a few months when the boys didn't see her at all. Eventually, they started visiting again, just a few hours a week, even during the pandemic. By then, though, the relationship had deteriorated. It wasn't one big incident that led to a breaking point. It was years of buildup, with every visit becoming a source of stress for them. She would yell, lose her temper, and take out her frustrations on them.

A lot of her rage wasn't even about them. It was clear to me that she was directing her anger at everyone in her life—her family, her team—but the boys were caught in the crossfire. Every visit seemed to end with her yelling about something, whether it was about Jamie, work, or her frustrations with life in general. The boys just didn't want to deal with it anymore. They wanted to be teenagers. To hang out with their friends, play video games, focus on their own lives. Not get dragged into adult drama.

One recurring issue was her insistence on controlling how they looked. She wanted them to dress a certain way, often for social media photos, and it became a constant battle. The boys hated it. They didn't want to be her props, and they told her as much. They even told me they didn't want me to post pics of us on social media and I stopped the instant they asked. Jayden, especially, was tired of being spoken to like a baby. They asked her to stop, but she wouldn't. When they resisted, it would escalate into arguments, with her yelling at them for not complying.

Preston often retreated to his room during visits, isolating himself to avoid the tension. Jayden would sometimes try to play the piano to drown out the noise pollution. But even those attempts at escape didn't help much, as her anger would seep into everything. When they came home, they were emotionally drained. And this after spending only a couple of hours with her.

On top of that, there were the lies. She constantly bad-mouthed me in front of them, calling me lazy, a piece of shit, and claiming I was taking all her money. The boys, who lived with me full-time, saw the reality of my life and couldn't reconcile it with what she was saying. They pushed back, telling her they didn't believe her and that they didn't want to hear her talk about me like that. It was hard for them to process. She was their mom, after all. They wanted to love her and respect her, but they were being bombarded with negativity and lies, while I never once bad-mouthed her to them.

She also spoke poorly about her own friends and family in front of them. They heard her vent about her dad, about Jodi—the professional conservator who took over from him and, in my view, did a helluva job—and about anyone else she felt wronged her. Her ranting was relentless. She blamed everyone for everything. I tried to shield the boys from it all, but I wasn't the one perpetuating the toxicity. Someone on her side should have sat them down and explained the truth about what was happening. Instead, they were left confused, trying to piece together a coherent narrative from the conflicting stories they were being told.

Eventually, I had to sit Preston and Jayden down myself. They were around thirteen or fourteen, old enough to hear the truth, or at least as much of it as I could give them. I told them everything—from the reasons for our divorce to the details of the conservatorship and its complexities. It was hard, but it was necessary. They needed to understand that not everything they heard from their mom was accurate. They needed to know that they could ask me anything and I would tell them the truth. Even if it made me look bad.

I also explained the conservatorship to them, including how she could have petitioned to end it if she had felt ready to take control of her life. That it lasted for thirteen years was a reflection of her struggles.

For years, she placed blame on everyone but herself—me, her father, her team. The boys grew up hearing this, and it left them confused and frustrated. They didn't want to pick sides or be caught in the middle, but they felt like they had no choice. They love their mom, but they couldn't deal with the environment she created. Over time, their visits had become less frequent, then stopped altogether.

It wasn't a sudden decision. It was the result of years of feeling unheard, manipulated, and dragged into drama they didn't want any part of. They just wanted to be kids, and I couldn't blame them for that. As much as I wanted them to have a relationship with their mom, I couldn't force them into a situation that was clearly causing them harm.

When the boys finally made the decision not to go back to their mom's house, everything changed. They had not been doing overnights for some time now, but even the few hours a week wasn't working either. I think they'd wanted to tell me for a while but didn't know how. When they finally said it—"We're not going back to mom's anymore"—you could feel the tension in our house evaporate. They weren't bouncing between two worlds anymore. They could finally breathe.

After that, they really started to come into their own. I gave them space to do their thing: go hang out with friends, catch Ubers across town, just be normal high school kids. Jayden even decided he wanted to go to public school. And man, right away, Vic and I could see the difference. Preston seemed way less anxious. He seemed more comfortable in his own skin, like he was finally stepping out of the shell he'd lived in for so long.

Preston had always been the quieter one, but he started opening up, hanging with friends, riding around, making young memories. It wasn't like he was rushing into the crazy side of high school. He just found his circle, his people, and it gave him a new kind of confidence. He started to shine in a way I hadn't seen before.

Jayden was finding his lane too, diving deep into music. He got this opportunity to mess around in the school band room, even though he couldn't read music. They had a soundproof piano room, and the teachers would just let him go in there and play during class. He'd taught himself back in sixth grade, picking it up by ear, figuring out how to express himself without needing sheet music in front of him. Watching that happen was like seeing a whole new side of him unfold.

Early on, I started showing them the basics of home music production. I bought them some simple software, taught them how to make beats, how to build a track from scratch. Once they got the hang of it, I brought in some of my producer friends— some EDM guys, some hip-hop heads—to work with them once or twice a week. Just a few hours here and there, but it was planting seeds.

We eventually found a high school with a one-on-one structure and a Recording Arts program—perfect for them. They started learning how to build real songs, understand music on a deeper level. Music became their escape, their safe space, much more than a hobby. It was therapy. Whenever the weight of everything with their mom crept in—questions, hurt, confusion—they could get lost in their creativity. It gave them peace when nothing else really could. It was their way of dealing, coping, healing.

And now, all that time they put in is starting to pay off. Jayden's making records, and if you heard the stuff he's working on, you'd be blown away. Same with Preston. He's brought tracks to me that are absolute bangers and over the years learned how to play guitar. Both of them have different paths they want to take, but music will always be part of their lives, whether it's production, sound design for films, whatever. They have a foundation now, something solid they built themselves.

I really believe that those few years of stability, just being under one roof, not bouncing back and forth, made all the difference. They got a nice start on figuring out who they are without all the drama. And there was plenty of that.

CHAPTER TWENTY-FOUR

W hen the conservatorship ended, I braced for the worst. With her newfound freedom, I saw history repeating itself.

Her social media posts became more erratic. There were the infamous videos of her dancing with knives, cryptic rants, and wild behavior that was impossible to ignore. It didn't take a rehab counselor to see that she was high in many of those videos.

The boys quickly learned to avoid social media altogether. They knew what it would bring: endless negativity and blame aimed at them from fans who didn't understand the full story. The Free Britney extremists were brutal. The boys understood that it was better to form a relationship with their mom on their own terms. They didn't need to read the hateful comments posted about their family, people calling them "liars," "traitors," "drama queens." Spitting out vile crap like: "What kind of son doesn't stand up for his own mother?" Or: "You'll regret turning your back on your mom when she's gone…" And those were some of the tamer comments.

Britney did nothing to stop the online hate aimed at her own sons. In fact, she only poured fuel on the fire with her own posts. She had nobody there that truly cares for her, to talk her off the ledge. She'd pushed away everyone who cared about her. Assistants, managers, security; she was cycling through people as fast as before, firing and replacing them. It felt like the same whirlwind we went through during our divorce, when nothing and no one around her stuck around for long.

The boys remained on edge. Jayden, especially, held onto the hope that he could be the difference-maker. He believed that if he said the right thing, she would listen to him. I didn't want to crush his hope; but the truth is, Britney hasn't been in a place to listen to anyone for years. Despite my best efforts to shield them, the emotional toll of Britney's behavior was unavoidable. I had spent years putting my life on hold, dedicating myself to ensuring the boys could have some semblance of a normal relationship with their mom. I stopped working and poured all my energy into providing stability for them. But no matter what I did, it felt impossible. Britney's narcissistic tendencies and her inability to take accountability for her actions consistently sabotaged progress.

One incident stands out as a breaking point. Shortly after we'd moved to Hawaii, Preston went on a vacation to Europe with his girlfriend's family. It was supposed to be a happy, carefree trip, but a phone call from Britney turned it into something else entirely. During their conversation, she started her usual routine, blaming me, her father, and the rest of her family for her problems.

Preston, to his credit, confronted her. He called out her lies and refused to accept her narrative. Her response was chilling: she told him she wished he, his brother, and me were all dead. Hearing Preston recount that conversation devastated me. How could a mother say that to her son? Preston, having dealt with her vitriol for years, took it better than I did. He understood her anger and instability, but it didn't make it any less painful. Trauma like that left scars, ones I fear they'll carry for the rest of their lives.

These weren't isolated incidents.

During Jayden's ninth-grade year at Calabasas High, Britney's messages disrupted his life again. She'd send him texts while he was in class, berating him and accusing him of being like me and her dad. The messages left him in tears, and I had to go pull him out of school to console him. It was just further proof of how her inability to take responsibility for her actions had bled into every corner of our lives.

Even after they cut off visits, the barrage continued. One day it was a soft check-in, "I miss you, baby." The next, a venom-fueled tirade. Britney cast herself as the victim and accused everyone else, including her own boys, of betrayal. Her refusal to acknowledge her role in what happened—losing custody, the conservatorship, and the strained relationships—was the root of everything. For almost twenty years now, not once has she ever genuinely apologized or admitted fault. It was always someone else's doing. Over the years, I've had to carefully guide the boys out of the mindset Britney tried to instill in them that everyone else was to blame for her problems. By the time they were teenagers, they had started to believe her narrative. It took countless conversations and a lot of patience to help them see the bigger picture. I never spoke badly about her; I simply presented the facts.

For example, when Britney claimed she was locked up and controlled, I'd ask them to reflect on the many trips she took or the freedom she had to make decisions. Yes, there were controls in place, but they weren't as severe as she made them out to be. The boys needed to understand that the conservatorship wasn't some grand conspiracy. It was a response to her actions. The truth wasn't easy to hear, but it was necessary for them to make sense of their reality.

While I was doing damage control behind the scenes, Britney's public behavior and outbursts only made things worse. She began posting old pictures of Preston and Jayden pretending they were current, to make it seem like everything was fine between them. It wasn't. They hadn't seen her in over two years. When Jayden did an interview to share his perspective, he was honest yet hopeful. He spoke about his love for his mom and his wish for her to get better so they could have a real relationship again.

Her response?

She trashed him on social media, told him to go read a book, called him out for being just like his grandfather if he didn't see things her way, and threw in a "sorry not sorry" for good measure. She publicly ridiculed his heartfelt gesture, and her fans happily piled on, backing her without hesitation and unleashing an all-out online assault on both Jayden and Preston. Grown adults targeting teenagers, chastising them to "respect your mother," branding them "ungrateful little shits."

It was brutal.

No matter how hard I tried to shield them, the damage was done.

They saw the comments, heard the accusations, and felt the weight of being vilified by their mom's followers. The lies were one thing, but it was her betrayal that hit hardest. They had stood by her through everything, hoping for a chance to reconnect, only to be publicly humiliated. It confirmed their worst fears about their mom's behavior. For them, it meant more than losing trust. It confirmed that the relationship they longed for might never happen.

Both boys have matured and gained a clearer perspective on their mom and the challenges she faces. They've also learned to protect themselves emotionally, knowing when to engage and when to step back.

As we've been working on this book, I've felt an increasing urgency that I can't ignore. The truth is, this situation with Britney feels like it's racing toward something irreversible. The signs are all there: the erratic behavior, the isolation, the cycling of people around her, the refusal to accept help. It's become impossible to pretend everything's okay. From where I sit, the clock is ticking, and we're getting close to the eleventh hour. Something bad is going to happen if things don't change, and my biggest fear is that our sons will be left holding the pieces. They love their mom. They've seen the red flags. But they don't know how to help without being attacked, misunderstood, or blamed.

What's made it so much harder is the fallout from the conservatorship. The Free Britney movement may have started from a good place, but it vilified everyone around her so intensely that now it's nearly impossible for anyone to step in. Judges, lawyers, even well-meaning professionals seem afraid to go near the situation, scared of the public backlash. I feel that leaves our boys stuck in the middle. They're watching their mom spiral, feeling powerless to stop it, and knowing that if they try, they'll be punished all over again. The world demanded Britney be left alone, but now that she's truly alone, nobody wants to face the consequences.

The Free Britney movement got it wrong. All those people who put so much effort into that should now put the same energy into the Save Britney movement. Because this is no longer about freedom. It's about survival.

I'm not saying I know the solution. But I do know that my sons can't carry this weight by themselves. They need support.

They need people to understand what's really going on, to listen, and to see this for what it is. This isn't some tabloid spectacle. It's a father's plea to everyone who has ever been moved by Britney. I'm asking the world: please stand by our sons and their mother. Now, more than ever, they need your support. I've been their buffer for years, but now it's bigger than me. It's time to sound the alarm.

As a father, I feel both pride and heartache. Pride in the resilience my sons have shown, and heartache for the burden they've had to bear. My focus remains the same: to give them the tools they need to navigate their relationship with their mom on their own terms, and to live their lives with as much peace and happiness as possible.

CHAPTER TWENTY-FIVE

I learned so much about raising a family from my own experiences as a kid. Growing up, my family dynamic was crazy, but it worked. My parents split when I was young, and both of them eventually remarried. So I ended up with four parents and a whole mess of siblings, seven of us in total. It was like some Brady Bunch shit, only a little rougher around the edges.

But even with all that, something amazing happened: everybody showed up. All four of my parents took the role of raising us seriously. Even if a kid wasn't their "blood," it didn't matter. They still parented. They made sure we were fed, clothed, disciplined, loved—and most importantly, taught how to be decent human beings who knew we were responsible for figuring life out on our own.

They didn't always get along. Sure, there were the usual tensions that come with blending families. But somehow, they made it work, even with five hundred miles between the two households. Nobody stepped on anyone else's toes. Everyone found their place in the system.

Each house had its own set of rules. At my dad's place, things were strict. My stepbrother and stepsister would get away with way more shit than I could. My dad had no problem laying down the hammer. He was terrified of waking up one day with the cops at his door because of something stupid we'd done. Me? I was grounded for half of my teenage life. Meanwhile, my older brother was out running wild, barely ever getting in trouble, even though he always got caught. It wasn't always fair, but it was still a family. A real one. We had each other's backs, no matter what.

I didn't realize it at the time, but all of that, watching four different parents make a broken situation feel whole, was preparing me for my own future. For having six kids with three different mothers. For figuring out how to build a family that didn't look perfect on paper but could still be solid where it mattered. It taught me that even when adult relationships didn't work out, the relationships with the kids still could.

I'm not saying everything was smooth in my own situation. Shit, we all know it wasn't. But I had a foundation to stand on. I knew I had to stay open, stay connected. I learned that from my mom. I didn't live with her, but I knew she was always just a phone call away. I could tell her anything growing up. She never judged, never ratted me out just to punish me. She gave me advice, real advice, and trusted me enough to let me make my own mistakes.

Same with my dad. Yeah, he'd ground my ass if I got caught doing something dumb, like the time he found a quarter-pound of weed stuffed in the pocket of my Raider jacket when I was in middle school. But he never made me feel like I couldn't come to him. Even when I screwed up, I knew I was still loved. Still welcome.

That's the kind of father I try to be today. I tell my kids all the time: Whatever it is—relationship problems, drugs, school, depression—come home. Talk to me. Don't ever feel like you have to deal with it alone. It doesn't matter if their moms and I aren't together. It doesn't matter how complicated life gets. What matters is that they know they're safe with me, no matter what.

That's the real gift my parents gave me. Not a perfect childhood. Not a perfect family. But a blueprint for how to love your kids through the mess, through the mistakes, through the real, raw parts of life.

The Spears family dynamic has always meant keeping the fasten seatbelt light on at all times, non-stop turbulence from takeoff to landing. And I think that pattern has never really shifted. Even when we were together, it was this constant pendulum swinging between anger and reconciliation. One moment, Britney wouldn't want to see anyone in her family, cutting them off completely. The next, she'd say how much she missed them and fly to Louisiana to make amends. But even then, the reconciliation rarely lasted long. Britney had this way of shutting out the world.

When I was first with her, it seemed like she was trying to protect our bubble; but over time, that bubble became suffocating. I thought it was about privacy, the paparazzi circus, the pressure of fame. But after years of nesting and isolating, it felt like there was something deeper at play. The pressure of being in the public eye created this invisible wall around her, one she couldn't, or wouldn't, let down.

Family visits were rare, almost nonexistent. My mom, my brother, my friends—they weren't allowed to just drop by or stay over. Even when our sons were born, her parents barely saw them. My family was practically barred from visiting. Coming from a big, family-oriented background, that was alien to me. Growing up, there was always someone around. Cousins, aunts, uncles, grandparents. Family was everything, and that's what I wanted for my kids.

But being with Britney meant that kind of connection was off the table. It wasn't just my family, either. Even her friends from back home were kept at arm's length. I brought it up with her occasionally. Not to argue, but out of concern. I wanted my boys to know their family, to feel that warmth of belonging. But for Britney, even a few hours with visitors felt like too much.

Everything was short-lived. Controlled.

It kept everyone on edge. Her family—especially her mom, her brother, and even her sister—spent years navigating that emotional minefield. They didn't want to risk being shut out, so they went along with it. Even when it meant compromising their own needs.

It became a vicious cycle.

Preston could stand his ground. Jayden struggled more. Even now, you feel it, the angst around how Britney might respond to any course of action.

Even with Britney's broader family, it was the same story. One day, she'd lash out. The next, she'd be vacationing in Mexico with her brother Bryan, or reconnecting with her mom. But these reunions always felt temporary, just another loop in the cycle.

I never got close to Bryan. To me, he's always been a wildcard. Britney had told me stories about them partying in the past. Ever since the night of my album release party I'd keep him at arm's length. He had his own struggles too. Living in the shadow of your sister's massive success isn't easy. Preston and Jayden love their Uncle Bryan. As they got older, he was someone they could talk to about life and guy shit. It made me happy to see that there was a good connection there, and came at a time when they really needed it.

Jamie, her dad, is a recovering alcoholic. I don't know if it's genetic or learned, but it had to have shaped Britney somehow. I've seen addiction in my own family. Some people dabble and walk away. Others get pulled under. I don't pretend to understand it fully, but I know it leaves deep scars. Out of everyone in her family, I was closest to Jamie by default. I've watched him navigate this whole situation and can honestly say I would never want to be in his shoes. Like the rest of us, Jamie is far from perfect, but he bears a heavy burden. He is the textbook definition of tough love. He has been put through the gauntlet of public opinion, something I am very familiar with, and never spoken badly about his daughter. That says everything.

The relationship between Britney and her dad was always unpredictable. They could go from calm to an all-out blowup in a heartbeat. Jamie was strict and old-school. He didn't pull punches when it came to discipline. Britney, on the other hand, could get physical when pushed. There was a private jet flight to Australia I didn't witness firsthand, but Lonnie, my security guy, was there. He told me Britney lost it mid-flight and hit Jamie so hard in the face, right in front of the boys, who were toddlers at the time. The boys freaked out. Lonnie took them to the back of the plane to get them out of harm's way and calm them down. The kids weren't the only ones rattled, so was Lonnie. Given the history between Britney and her father, it didn't shock me, but it was a sobering reminder of how combustible things could get between them. Britney got her temper from Jamie. That mix was like gasoline and fire.

Eventually, I had to file a restraining order against Jamie myself. It wasn't just one incident. This was the culmination of everything that had been building between the boys and their mom for years. It started when it was her turn with them and she dropped them off at Jamie's condo in Westlake. For a long time, things seemed fine with him. What I didn't know was that he'd started drinking again.

I was home when Jamie called, slurring his words, obviously drunk. I could hear a cocktail being mixed in the background as he launched into me out of nowhere. "You motherfucker, you want to take me to court?" he shouted. We'd butted heads before, but this was different—meaner, more erratic.

I tried to calm him down and figure out what the hell he was talking about. That's when he started ranting about something that happened with Preston.

They'd been eating dinner when Jamie started laying into Preston about playing sports, calling him lazy, telling him he needed to get into basketball. Preston was around thirteen at the time, already growing fast, already sensitive, and he didn't just sit there and take it. He mouthed off. Jamie snapped. Preston ran into the bedroom and locked the door. Jamie, in a rage, pounded on it, yelling, "Open this door or I'll break it down!" Preston didn't, and Jamie did exactly what he threatened.

There was a mirror on the other side of the door. When it shattered, glass flew everywhere. Thankfully, Preston had backed up. But Jamie stormed in, grabbed him by the shoulders, and started shaking him. He didn't hit him, but the damage was done. It was traumatizing.

As Jamie and I were speaking, Preston called. He FaceTimed me, crying, saying, "I don't ever want to see Pawpaw again." He was shaken. And this wasn't teenage drama. Preston had already been through more than any kid should have to. As if the emotional weight of his mom putting him down wasn't enough, now his grandfather had crossed a line too. Preston said he'd called his mom and she'd picked him and Jayden up. I asked her security to bring them straight to my house.

That night, after calming Preston down, I knew I couldn't just let it go. This had less to do with Jamie himself than a pattern that had to stop. Years of instability. The constant, creeping threat of harm. My job was to protect my sons. That line had been crossed. I called my lawyer, who told me to meet him at the Thousand Oaks police station the next morning.

We filed a report. Then we filed for a restraining order. It wasn't easy, but necessary. Jamie was drinking again, and I had lost trust in the situation. The restraining order was granted for three years. We got it done quickly. And yeah, part of me still wrestles with the length. Jamie knew he'd fucked up. I think he understood how serious it was. But I wasn't reacting to one outburst. I was responding to years of dysfunction and trauma. I knew he was sorry and felt horrible about the whole thing, but what was done was done. For years, I tried to maintain a fragile balance, keeping the peace, keeping relationships intact. But I realized sometimes the best way to protect your kids is to walk away from a toxic situation. I don't regret pulling the restraining order on Jamie, even if it caused a rift. My only regret is not seeing the damage for what it was, sooner.

The person I give the most respect to is Jamie Lynn. She had her own life, her own challenges, and her own take on the whole mess. After Britney got out of the conservatorship and began lashing out online, especially toward our boys, Jamie Lynn messaged my wife. And what she wrote gets me emotional every time: *Honestly, this makes me want to cry because I feel for those boys so much. I'm her little sister by ten years, and I can't imagine what her actual children must feel like at times, but I am familiar with the feeling of being a dingy trying to survive in a wave caused by another's ship, feeling like you have to rescue yourself. I always wanted her to get better, especially for the boys. I started to resent her for how she treated them because it was clearly affecting them. But in order to really get better, she would have to be honest and acknowledge the wrong she has done, as well as take accountability for certain circumstances, which she is incapable of doing. I'm still trying to come to terms with how she could be so unaware of anything outside of herself. I spent my whole life based around what was best for Britney, and I never wanted to step on any toes as the little sister, so I quietly built my own life and career. I tried to be supportive, but in a way that was healthy for my own well-being. I didn't want my girls to experience anything I did, but it looks like she wanted to make sure and attack what I created outside of her.*

Then, after purchasing a piano for Jayden as a Christmas gift, Jamie Lynn sent another message to my wife.

This one hit hard.

She wrote: *Jayden sent me the sweetest message about getting his piano, and it made my heart so happy to hear him so happy. I know I've said it so many times, but it's worth repeating—I'm so thankful the boys have had y'all to raise them to be well-mannered, appreciative, and kind boys. Any parent who's actually raised their children knows that raising kids is the toughest job on earth, and you both are raising those boys and their siblings while also having to constantly protect and shield them from so much chaos that no one would ever understand unless they lived through it. I don't think there's enough money or material things in the world that would be enough to repay y'all for doing what she couldn't be bothered to do as a parent. And I'm sure my sister has never thanked y'all for raising her children and still being beyond gracious to allow her so many chances to take part in their lives, even when y'all had more than enough reasons to validate cutting that off. So I wanted y'all to know how much you are appreciated and supported by those of us who love those boys.*

Jamie Lynn has always been cordial with me. I've known her since she was thirteen. As far as I'm concerned, she's the one person in the family who can truly relate to what Preston and Jayden have been through. Like them, she had to navigate the dysfunction at a young age. Jamie Lynn worked hard to build her own career. She landed *Zoey 101* at thirteen, and carved a career for herself outside of Britney's shadow. But even that became a sore spot. Britney wanted credit for Jamie Lynn's success, too.

That sense of entitlement ran through the family. One minute they were banished, the next they were welcomed back. I would give up my own time with Preston and Jayden just so Britney's side of the family could spend time with them, because she wouldn't let them see the boys on her time. It was important to me that the boys spend time with her family. Jamie Lynn, though, was different. She'd been through a lot and came out standing. And when she bought Jayden the piano that one Christmas, it wasn't the price-tag that made it special—it was that she understood what he needed. Seeing him light up over that gift meant more than she probably knows.

Which brings me to Britney's mom, Lynne.

Lynne has always struck me as someone with a huge heart and the best of intentions. Her love for her kids is undeniable. But she walks on eggshells around Britney. Always has. Since day one, I felt it. She would tiptoe through every conversation, afraid to trigger something. You could see it in her body language. Hear it in her voice.

I don't think Lynne is a villain in any of this. She's been caught in the middle—between loving her daughter and surviving her daughter. When things blew up in public, you could see it crush her. She cared deeply about what people thought, and she internalized everything. I think it wore her down.

During the worst of it, Lynne and Jamie Lynn kept in touch with Vic more than me, asking about the boys, sending gifts, trying to stay connected however they could. I never took it personally. I think they were just doing the best they could. There's always been a cloud over Lynne about the intervention stuff. Britney blames her for leading it. Maybe she did, maybe she didn't. But if she did, it was out of love. That doesn't make her the bad guy.

From my perspective, Lynne's just a mom trying to hold it all together—gracefully, painfully, and without a lot of thanks. She gets stepped on and still shows up. That's who I see when I look at her. Not the source of the problem, but someone doing her best in a situation where there are no easy answers.

EPILOGUE

Managing relationships across three families has proven one of the hardest challenges of my life. For me, it's about focusing on being a father to all of my children, navigating the unique dynamics of each situation, balancing their needs, and trying to make decisions that are right for everyone, while accepting that no solution will ever be perfect.

When Shar and I split, Kori and Kaleb were still so young that I told myself the timing might actually make it easier on them. Kaleb hadn't even been born yet, and Kori was just shy of two. I convinced myself that stepping away early meant they wouldn't remember what it was like to have both parents under one roof. That maybe, in some way, it was cleaner—less damaging. But I've come to understand it doesn't work like that. Even if kids can't remember the specifics, they still feel the absence. They still carry the weight.

Kori and Kaleb had an incredible mom in Shar. I always knew they were being raised right, with love, stability, and a strong foundation. But during those early, whirlwind years with Preston and Jayden, I knew my role had to look different. Their world was volatile—surrounded by cameras, headlines, courtrooms. They needed me in a way that required everything I had. I had to be their constant, their anchor. Meanwhile, Shar and I didn't live close, so seeing Kori and Kaleb meant long drives, packing bags, juggling holidays and weekends. I made the effort every time, because I wanted them to know I was there. Still, as they got older, things got more complicated. Kaleb, especially, felt the difference. He saw the time and energy I gave to Preston and Jayden, and even though I tried to explain, to reassure him, I could see it created something in him I couldn't quite fix. I thought I was doing the right thing. I hope someday they'll understand why it played out the way it did.

One thing I'm proud of is how close all my kids have stayed. That didn't happen by accident. It took effort, planning, and a lot of intention. I made sure they were together as much as possible, whether it was summer vacations, weekends, or special trips, always prioritizing opportunities for them to bond. Even now, they talk every day, play video games together, and look out for one another like true siblings.

I've been blessed with six incredible children, each with their own unique personality, dreams, and challenges. My firstborn, Kori, now twenty-three, was my crash course in parenthood, an overwhelming wake-up call no book could prepare me for. I was the dad checking her breathing at night, nervous and protective to a fault. She's always been an angel, easygoing and thoughtful, with an old-soul energy that avoids drama. Passionate about gaming, anime, and Japanese culture, she dreams of visiting Japan, and I'm determined to make that happen soon.

Kaleb, twenty-one, is my mirror with his charming, rebellious spirit. He made me a grandfather recently. A shock at first, to say the least. But I'm so proud of how Kaleb's stepping into fatherhood. He's always been driven, whether it's football, martial arts, or his dream of rapping, and I'll keep supporting him as he follows his path.

Preston, twenty, is my thinker and deep feeler, a steady, calm presence with a sharp creative mind and a love for music. His bond with his brother Jayden, now nineteen, is beyond strong. They've been best friends since they were little, facing life's challenges as a team. Jayden's my firecracker, bold, expressive, and brimming with creative energy. As a kid, he'd roar like a dinosaur or mimic sound effects with uncanny precision, and now that charisma fuels his passion for music. Watching them grow as each other's biggest supporters has been one of my greatest joys.

Jordan, fourteen, is the sweetheart, curious, adventurous, and full of life. She's a dancer, instantly transforming into a confident, captivating performer the moment she hits the stage. And dedicated. Her dance company has won national awards. She's driven, doing it her way, brushing off my old dance videos with a knowing smile, but I'm just happy to guide her from the sidelines.

Peyton, eleven, is our little spark, playful, curious, fearless. She's the loudest and toughest, taking broken bones and stitches in stride, with a sharp tongue and a gut punch for anyone who crosses her. Her energy reminds me of Jayden at that age, dramatic, hilarious, and always the center of attention in the best way. As the youngest, she's carved her own space, surrounded by love from her siblings.

The bond between them all wouldn't exist without the work Vic and I put in to keep everyone together. It wasn't always easy, especially with so many moving parts and competing priorities, but it was worth it. Vic helped me see the bigger picture, and that changed everything for the better. One thing has never wavered: I know I've been a great father. That's the single biggest thing I take pride in.

Living in Hawaii has always been a dream, one that seemed distant and unattainable for so long. For over twenty years, I would visit, and every time I left, it got harder to leave. The island has always had a pull on me, offering a sense of peace and simplicity that felt like the exact opposite of everything I experienced back in Los Angeles. Finally making the move felt like a breath of fresh air, a chance to start over and live in a way that felt more grounded and true.

After everything in L.A.—the pace, the pressure, the noise—I needed a reset. Here in Hawaii, it feels like I've finally gotten my life back. People don't care who you are. There's no paparazzi waiting to jump out of the bushes, no cameras tracking my kids' every move. It's a relief to not have to constantly look over my shoulder, and that freedom has been a game-changer for all of us.

Even for my kids, this place has been transformative. It's a different vibe out here, a community that feels safer and more supportive. They can go out and explore without the kinds of worries that followed us in L.A. Jayden has already returned to L.A., chasing his music dreams, and Preston is finding his way as an adult. Watching both of them grow into themselves has filled me with pride. We've done everything we could to prepare them for life, and I know they're ready.

Hawaii has become the perfect home base for our family. I know the kids will always come back here, even if they don't settle down on the island themselves. They know that we're here for them whenever they need it, and that kind of stability is something I've worked hard to provide. As I sit here now, looking out at the ocean, I feel a sense of contentment I haven't felt in years. Life isn't perfect—whose is?—but it feels manageable in a way it didn't before. Hawaii has given me the space to breathe, to reconnect with myself and my family, and to find a sense of balance.

For the first time in a long time, I feel like I'm exactly where I'm meant to be. And no matter how far we've come or how different our lives may look now, the truth is that my bond with my kids is permanent. It doesn't fade with time or distance. Even now, as they step into adulthood, there are still moments when they need support, guidance, or just someone to show up. And when those moments come, I do what I've always done—show up for them in the ways I know how. That's the role I've committed to, and it doesn't end just because they're getting older. By finally speaking about all of this, after nearly two decades, I hope it brings healing. Not just for me, but for the people I love. We can't change the past, but maybe we can make peace with it. Maybe we can let it rest.

ACKNOWLEDGMENTS

To my parents: Mike, Collette, Julie, and Coby. I don't know if I've ever truly thanked you, so let me say it here. Thank you for the good times and the tough ones. Thank you for showing up, for the sacrifices, for the discipline, and for the lessons. Thank you for listening, caring, teaching, and believing in me. You each gave me tools that shaped who I am. You're the reason I'm the father I am today, and that's the greatest gift a parent can give. I love you all.

Victoria, every road I've walked has led me to you. Thank you for your love, patience, and strength.

To my siblings: Dustin, Nikki, Chris, Patrick, Camron, and Kurtis. Thank you for the foundation, the sense of belonging, and all the moments in between.

Chris Federline, thank you for the wild adventures, your fearlessness, and for always showing up when it counted.

To my mother-in-law Brenda, thanks for always keeping it real. I only hope my children speak about me the same way your daughter does about you. Love you

Jimmy Federico, thank you for helping me find my path and for being there through every step of it.

Marty Kudelka, thank you for showing me what I was capable of.

Eddie Morales, thank you for believing in me.

Big Mike, thank you for always looking out. You've been solid since day one.

You're all my brothers, and I'm grateful to have gone through life with you by my side.

Jay Anderson, thank you for being a real one and for the beats.

Seo, A.L., Kayes, B. Jones, and all my New York fam—rest in peace, Mike Williams. Your spirit still motivates me.

Lonnie Jones, thank you for always being there for my family. I'm proud to call you my brother.

To my nanny, Jenny McCarthy—there are no words to express how thankful I am for you. You held everything together in my darkest hour. I believe God brought you into our lives right when we needed you. We love you.

Jamie and Lynne Spears, thank you for always putting the boys first.

Jamie Lynne, thank you for being such a strong and loving role model to your nephews.

Joey Granath, thank you for the laughs and for standing beside me through everything.

Mark Kaplan, thank you for being a bulldog and fighting for what was right. You never backed down.

Todd Dukes, Big Dog, Big E (rest in peace), Rob, and the entire security crew. You're more than protection. You're family.

Nina Nisenholtz, thank you for sticking it out with me for over twenty years. That loyalty means everything.

Brendan Filuk, thank you for seeing something in me early on and giving me the chance to prove myself.

Scott Storch, Damon Thomas, Rich Rocka, 1500, James Fauntleroy, Jukebox, Crichy, Styles and Complete, CJ, Deezle — and everyone else who worked on music that never got released — thank you for the studio memories. And thank you to those of you who helped teach my sons how to make music. That's something they'll carry for life.

To everyone who's played a role in my life and isn't mentioned here, thank you. I appreciate you.

A very special thank you to my publisher Jaren Hayman, my editor Alex Holstein, and the whole Listenin team for helping me tell this story and bringing it to life.

To my children:

Go out and explore this life. Live it fully. Chase your dreams. Don't chase money. True happiness comes from within, and no amount of fame or fortune can replace that. When life gets hard — and it will — keep your head up and learn from the struggle. Let yourself fall. Let yourself get back up. It won't be easy, but it will be worth it.

From the moment each of you were born, you changed my purpose. You are the most incredible and fulfilling parts of my life. I am proud every single day to be your father.

And I will always be with you. The tattoo on my arm says, "My blood runs through your veins. That is an unbreakable bond in life and a spiritual connection in death. I am part of you."

We are forever connected. I love you.

b8c81a90-6e79-43b6-9d11-1debcf679940R01